100 great **pasta** dishes

Ann and Franco Taruschio

100 great pasta dishes

with photographs by **Ray Main**

Kyle Cathie Limited

To Jack our grandson, aged seven, who loves
eating pasta – even for breakfast.

Editor Sheila Davies

Copy Editor Linda Doeser

Editorial Assistant Sarah Epton

Designer Mark Latter at Vivid Design

Photograper Ray Main

Home Economist Janie Suthering

Stylist Helen Trent

Production by Lorraine Baird and Sha Huxtable

First published in Great Britain 2002 by
Kyle Cathie Limited, 122 Arlington Road, London NW1 7HP

ISBN 1 85626 463 7

A Cataloguing In Publication record for this title is available from the
British Library.

Colour separations by Colourscan, Singapore
Printed and bound by Star Standard, Singapore

 = VEGETARIAN

 = VEGAN

Contents

Introduction by Ann Taruschio

This pasta book offers recipes collected and used by us from various regions of Italy, as well as favourite recipes given to us by family and friends. Some of them are quite complicated, but there are also some extremely simple ones. None of the recipes is beyond the capability of the average cook and, certainly, none requires the skill of a chef with a brigade of assistants. All of them can be made in a domestic kitchen. Some of the recipes come from Franco's home region, the Marche, until recently a little known area of Italy. Marche is on the Adriatic coast of Italy, bordered by Emilia-Romagna, Tuscany, Umbria and Abruzzi. Food from the sea, the plain, the hills and the mountains is plentiful. To go to the local meat, game, fish, dairy, fruit and vegetable markets is amazing – a real eye-opener.

When our daughter Pavinee was younger, I used to spend summer holidays on the beach in Italy. During the week, the beach was populated mostly by women and children and while the children played, the women chatted. They were mostly professionals, but I never heard them talking about their jobs. Their conversations always centred on food and their families. They discussed where to buy the best produce, swapped recipes, debated the ideal way to cook a particular fish and so on. When they learned that, despite being English, I was also interested in food and that my husband and I were researching a book on bruschetta, recipes for bruschetta came flooding in. My notebook was quickly filled and then they started to talk about baked pastas (*pasta al forno*). Some of these women, although originally Marchigiani (people who hail from the Marche) had married Italians from away and so brought with them recipes from other regions. In the UK we are still quite limited when we think of making a baked pasta at home, but there's a wealth of dishes to choose from. Each day, I would listen to descriptions of the pasta dish they had prepared for the evening meal. Sometimes it was a baked pasta that just needed putting in the oven on the return from the evening's *passagiata*. At other times, it was a sauce which had already been prepared and just needing reheating and adding to quickly boiled pasta. The *passagiata*, by the way, is the evening promenade up and down the *corso*, or main street, between six and seven in the evening. It never fails to amuse me – the beach empties at four o'clock and we are left alone. Then, out they come at six, all smartly dressed, and, like migratory birds, all disappear again at seven, only to reappear at ten for a cup of coffee and a digestif or, even later, an ice cream.

I used to feel guilty when the women talked about being at the fish market at the crack of dawn, when the fishing boats came in. Sometimes they bought fish to serve after the pasta, simply cooked on the barbecue with a touch of olive oil, plenty of lemon juice and salt. Or, perhaps, they bought vongole, clams, to make spaghetti con vongole – so fresh, so perfect. With a platter of cured meats and griddled vegetables to start or follow, a salad of herbs and various leaves and a bowl of fresh fruit still warm from the sun, they made a perfect meal. Why feel guilty? 'Get up and join them,' I thought and so I, too, became an early bird.

According to our daughter, my sister-in-law, Rita, makes the best pasta – her tagliatelle with duck and pea sauce is perfect and her vincisgrassi di carne, baked pasta with meat, is a dream. Daughter and now grandson, Jack, would feel very cheated if they were not invited to share a plate of Rita's pasta each time they are in Italy. If it's a boiled pasta, we have to be sure to be at the table promptly. Like her mother before her, Rita puts the hand-rolled, thin, yellow strands of tagliatelle into the water only once we are all seated. Jack, at the age of five, on being asked whether Rita's or Franco's pasta was better, replied diplomatically, 'They are both the same because they are brother and sister'.

One of the great things about the Italians is that they have a tremendous respect for the gifts of nature and treat food with love and simplicity. They love food, love cooking and love the people for whom they cook. Everything is done with a passion. They are proud of their culinary heritage. Through the following recipes and anecdotes we hope to take the reader and cook on a journey around various regions of Italy. Above all, we want to convey that cooking does not necessarily mean stressfully trying to emulate celebrity chefs. It can mean reproducing recipes that people have been cooking for centuries all over Italy. These recipes have a background and soul. They talk to us of Italy, past and present.

The origins of pasta

We know that the ancient Greeks, Romans and Etruscans all cooked a rudimentary form of pasta. The Greeks cooked a pasta they called *laganon* and the Romans *lagani*. A relief in the Etruscan tombs at Ceveteri, north of Rome, shows a large table with raised sides, on which servants mix flour with water. A jug, ladle, rolling pin and cutting wheel stand in the foreground. It seems logical to conclude that these were implements to be used for making pasta.

We know for sure that the Sicilians were making pasta as early as the twelfth century, long before Marco Polo went to

China. In the book of *Ruggero* (from the name of the Norman ruler of Sicily who commissioned the work), the twelfth-century Arab writer Idrisi writes:

'West of Termini [Imerese] we come to the village of Trabia, an enchanting place, rich in waters and mills, that faces a beautiful plain punctuated by farms, where spaghetti are produced in such quantities that they not only meet the needs of the people of Calabria [all of southern Italy] but are also exported throughout Muslim and Christian lands.' Maccheroni, dried pasta, was first used by the Sicilians. They were influenced by the Arabs, who dried noodles so that they could be used by nomads. The Arabs introduced Sicily and southern Italy to the art of forming strands of pasta with a hollow centre, so that it dried thoroughly. In a seventeenth-century comedy, a Sicilian is contemptuously dismissed by his

Neapolitan rival in love as a *mangia-maccheroni*, or macaroni-eater. The Sicilian retaliates by calling the Neapolitan, a *sporco-foglie*, a dirty leaf-eater, referring to the leaves of pasta that the Neapolitans use to prepare their much-loved pasticcio.

In the *mezzogiorno* of Italy, the southern regions, macaroni is now the generic term for all commercially made dried pasta. In the north of Italy, macaroni refers specifically to a short, ribbed tubular pasta. Where does the term macaroni come from? The dictionary says 'origin unknown' but it could come from the Latin *macerare*, which means to mix or knead. There is a charming fable that tells how the word macaroni came to be. A Neapolitan prince, on trying the new pasta and hearing how costly it was to make, exclaimed '*Si buoni ma caroni*!' – so good but so expensive.

Another fable went around Vecchia Napoli some 150 years ago. Matilde Seao wrote a book on the legends of Naples about this time and included the following story, setting the date for the event as 1220. A man known as the Magician Chico lived in a house in the Via dei Cortellari, People could see him stirring large pots and used to pass his house with fear. What was he stirring? Nobody knew! Chico had once been wealthy but had fallen on hard times and been deserted by all his friends. Far from becoming disgruntled and bitter, he devoted himself to discovering the secret of happiness for humankind. Then, Jovanella, a nosy neighbour, managed to spy on Chico and discovered what he was doing. Her husband was employed by Federico II, so she asked him to tell the emperor that she possessed the secret of a food that would make all

men happy. The emperor sent his cook to Jovanella's house, where she prepared the dish as only a Neapolitan can. The emperor rewarded her richly for her precious discovery and everyone – nobles and ordinary citizens alike – flocked to her door. Jovanella became rich. Then Chico, on one of his rare outings, smelt a familiar and divine smell and knew his secret had been stolen. That day, he disappeared, never to be seen again. Jovanella continued to live happily until the hour of her death, when she confessed her crime and died in terror of eternal torment.

The locals used to say that if you passed the house of Mago Chico on a Saturday night at the right hour, you might see him cutting his macaroni into lengths, Jovanella chopping the tomatoes to make the sauce and the Devil himself grating the cheese with one hand, while he fanned the flue with the other. It is an amusing legend, but one thing ruins it – tomatoes did not arrive in Italy for at least another 300 years.

To make pasta using a hand machine

When we make pasta with a hand machine or entirely by hand, we use Farina 0. This flour is obtainable from Italian delicatessens. If you cannot find it, use strong plain white flour instead. Farina 00 is better for electric pasta machines.

Basic Pasta Dough

350g (12oz) Farina 0 or strong plain white flour
3 eggs
salt

Put the flour in a mound on a work surface, then make a hollow in the centre. Add a little salt to the eggs, beat lightly with a fork and then pour them into the hollow. Draw the flour

into the eggs until it is well amalgamated. If the mixture is too moist, add a little more flour.

On a clean area of the work surface, knead the dough with the heel of your hand, keeping your fingers bent, folding the pasta in half and giving it a half-turn. Do this for 10 minutes.

This process can also be done in a food processor or, after the initial amalgamation, the pasta dough can be rolled through the rollers of a pasta machine set at maximum width. Do this four or five times or until the pasta is smooth.

Thin the pasta progressively until the desired thickness is reached, according to the type of pasta you are making (consult the manufacturer's handbook for guidelines). Cover any pasta that is not being rolled with cling film. As the pasta is done, lay it on clean teacloths. Leave to dry for 1 hour before boiling.

If you follow the simple rule of using good-quality flour and the best eggs you can find, home-made pasta cannot fail. The eggs must be absolutely fresh and a good way to test them is to put them in salted, cold water. If they sink, they are fresh (up to 3 days old); if they float halfway up, they are 3–6 days old; if they rise to the top, they are stale.

We hope these recipes will take the fear out of pasta making, which can be very therapeutic. Bought fresh pasta is, of course, permitted, but combining home-made pasta with home-made sauces creates a perfect balance of flavours that can only be achieved by the cook who follows the recipe from beginning to end.

Hints on cooking pasta

Use a pan that is deeper than it is wide.
Allow 1 litre (1¾ pints) of water for every 100g (3½oz) of pasta, and a pinch of salt for every 1 litre (1¾ pints) of water. Add the pasta and salt to the water only when it is boiling hard. Do not put olive oil in the cooking water, it will only make the sauce slip off the pasta as you eat it. Simply stir the pasta often during cooking to prevent it from sticking. Fresh

pasta takes only a few minutes to cook – watch it carefully and drain the pasta when it is al dente – firm, but not crunchy.

With home-made pasta sheets for lasagne or cannelloni, cook a few sheets at a time. You will know they are ready when they rise to the surface of the boiling water. Don't allow them to over-cook as they will be re-cooked later.

Pasta tips

If you have sheets of home-made pasta left-over, these should be individually wrapped and can be kept in the freezer for up to 3 months.

If you want to use dried pasta and the recipe specifies fresh, remember that 100g (3½oz) dried pasta is the equivalent of 150g (5oz) fresh pasta.

A good tip for serving pasta, particularly baked or layered dishes, is to leave the pasta to rest for 10 minutes after cooking. This makes it easier to cut and serve, as the layers hold together. As the dish is baked in the oven, it retains its heat even if left to stand.

As far as dried pasta is concerned, as a general rule, the higher the price, the better the quality, so it pays to buy the best.

You will note that modern, coloured pastas, such as tomato (red), beetroot (magenta), cuttlefish or squid ink (black) and wild mushroom (brown), have not been used in these recipes. This is because in authentic, traditional Italian cooking, these varieties are not normally used. However, there's nothing to stop you from experimenting – chocolate-flavoured pasta, for example, is great with game recipes.

Pasta, served with a sauce offers everything the body needs from the nutritional point of view – carbohydrate from the pasta and protein and fibre from the sauce. Where protein may be lacking, a sprinkling of grated Parmesan cheese makes up the difference. With the addition of a salad, you have a perfectly balanced meal. However, for authenticity, you should always eat your salad after your pasta and not with it.

The etiquette of eating spaghetti

Galateo, written by Giovanni Della Casa between 1551 and 1555, and published posthumously in Venice in 1558, was a book on social behaviour. The word '*Galateo*' is used in Italy to mean that someone's manners may not be quite correct. *Non conosce il Galateo* – he does not know his *Galateo*. In 1958, I attended Corsham Court Bath Academy of Art. The then principal, Clifford Ellis, requested we should all read *Galateo* as our Christmas reading matter. He informed us that the writings were as true today as when they were first published. I wonder if we all improved after reading it.

I remember Franco, in the 1960s, rushing into the bar of our restaurant and catching sight of a lady struggling with a plate of spaghetti. She was wearing a fur coat with a large collar and was perched on a bar stool at the counter. He stopped in his tracks and said, 'Excuse me, Madam, in my country we remove our coats when we eat and we twist the pasta'. I nearly died of embarrassment. Every time I see an old postcard of the street urchins in long-ago Naples eating spaghetti with their fingers, tipping their heads slightly back and dropping the spaghetti into their mouths, I think of the struggling fur-clad lady.

Spaghetti should be eaten only with a fork, never with a spoon and fork; that is considered very bad form. Do not hold the fork vertically and twist; hold it lightly inclined towards the horizontal, then twist.

The history of the table fork with two tines can be traced back to the time of the ancient Greeks. In the seventh century AD, royal courts in the Middle East began to use forks at the table. Between the tenth and thirteenth centuries, forks were fairly common among the elite of Byzantium and in the eleventh century, the Greek wife of a Venetian Doge, Domenico Selvo, brought forks to Italy. When she died not long after her marriage, the Venetians, who were scandalised by the use of the fork, perceived her death as divine justice.

However, it was not until the sixteenth century that forks really caught on in Italy. In 1608, the Englishman Thomas Coryate, known as Furcifer, the fork-bearer, brought the first forks to England after seeing them on his travels in Italy. These forks still only had two long tines.

A moment of glory for spaghetti happened in Naples between 1837 and 1847. King Ferdinand II was a young man of strong character who loved progress. Until that period, spaghetti had been eaten with the fingers and was considered food for the plebs. The king loved spaghetti, but was forced to deny himself the pleasure of a plate of his favourite food when he had important guests. The fork in use at that time had three, long prongs, which often stabbed the eaters in the mouth. The

Lord Chamberlain, Gennaro Spadiccini, heard the king's complaints about stabbing himself so many times that he decided to invent a better fork. He came up with the idea of creating a fork with four short prongs, which is still in use today. Even in the early 1900s the *lazzaroni*, street urchins, of Naples still used their fingers to eat their spaghetti.

Eating pasta

Some of the recipes in this book constitute a meal in themselves, for example the timballi and pasticci. In Italy, they would be followed by a *contorno* which might be a salad of some description – green, mixed or tomato – cooked spinach tossed with extra virgin olive oil and a touch of garlic and chilli or perhaps a plate of French beans dressed with chopped anchovies, garlic, parsley and olive oil. The contorno is always eaten after the pasta. Other pasta dishes can either be eaten before the main meal or as a main meal, depending on your appetitite.

Olive oil

Olive oil has been used in Mediterranean countries for thousands of years, but it has only recently become so popular outside these countries. This is partly the result of the discovery that it protects us against diseases of the heart and arteries. It is also rich in vitamin E, which slows down the ageing process of the skin and bones.

Olive oil is the only oil made from a whole fruit and olive trees, with their gnarled and twisted trunks and magnificent, silvery green foliage, are symbolic of strength, faith and peace. There is a story in the Old Testament that a dove sent out from the Ark returned with an olive branch in its beak, which was said to be a sign that peace had been made between man and nature. Together with bread and wine, olive oil and olives are an integral part of Italian life. There is an Italian saying that goes: 'What love, olive oil and wine can't cure, God help you.'

A little word of advice: olive oil must always be stored in a cool, dark place in the kitchen, otherwise it quickly goes rancid.

We often buy olive oil from the Santa Casa estate in Loreto in the Marche. The man in charge of the estate keeps all the details of the olive harvest written in copperplate in a leather-bound ledger. He writes down the type of olive picked, which fields they came from, which way the fields face, the time of day they were picked, whether there was a wind blowing at the time of picking and even which direction it blew from. If it blew from the sea, for example, there is a different flavour to the oil. Every minute detail is recorded and has been for hundreds of years.

The Santa Casa, the Holy House of Loreto, is situated inside Loreto's Basilica. This house is said to be where Mary the mother of Jesus received the news of her divine maternity. There is a statue of the Black Madonna of Loreto within the Santa Casa – black because the statue, which replaced the original cedarwood statue, darkened by age and dense oil smoke and destroyed by fire in 1921, has been given a light coating of black paint. The story goes that to prevent its destruction by the Turks, the house was miraculously raised and

transported from Palestine, first to Tersatto near Fiume in Croatia in 1291, then to Recanati in 1294 and, finally, to Loreto in 1295, where the sanctuary stands today. It is recorded that the event was accompanied by miracles and, from that time, people have travelled there from all over the world, hoping for a cure, just as they do to Lourdes.

Tomato

There is a little story from Romagna which goes as follows. There was once a priest who was always poking his nose into other people's affairs, not with malice – just simple curiosity. His parishioners, who were nevertheless very fond of him, nicknamed him Don Pomodoro (Don Tomato) because, like the tomato, he was into everything.

The tomato belongs to the same family as potatoes, peppers and aubergines. It was brought to Europe from the Americas in the sixteenth century. In 1554, botanist Pietro Andrea Mattioli from Siena was the first Italian to write about it. He gave a description of the fruit, which was originally yellow in colour, and named it *Mala aurea* (Latin) and *pomo d'oro* – golden apple. He remarked that tomatoes were to be cooked like aubergines, fried in olive oil with salt and pepper. Not long afterwards, Mattioli was writing about a red variety of tomato. For a long time in Italy, the tomato was confused with the aubergine. In fact, Antonio Nebbia in his cook book *Il Cuoco Maceratese*, 1784, gave a recipe for tomato sauce in which he stated that in the Marche, the tomato was called aubergine. It was not until the second half of the eighteenth century that the tomato started to appear in Italian recipes for sauces and it was still later, in the 1830s, that the alliance of pasta and tomatoes was created. This was followed in the second half of the nineteenth century by that other famous alliance of tomatoes and pizza.

The earliest known recipe for tomato sauce comes from a Neapolitan cook book *Lo Scalco alla moderna* by Antonio Latini, 1692–94. Spanish-style tomato sauce was made from finely chopped parsley, onion and garlic with salt, pepper, oil and vinegar added to the finely chopped flesh of previously seared and peeled tomatoes. Another tomato sauce for pasta appears in Ippolito Cavalcanti's *Cucina Teorico Pratica*, written in 1839.

We usually use plum tomatoes in our recipes. They are readily available during the summer months in Britain, but less so in winter months, when ordinary – usually under ripe and tasteless – tomatoes seem to dominate the greengrocers' shelves. Buy the tomatoes before you need them and allow them to ripen off. Always use tomatoes that are as red and ripe as possible.

Passata (Tomato Sauce)

This is a little tip for making passata. The act of sizzling the tomatoes brings out the natural sugar in them and slightly caramelises it, thus sweetening the rather dull tomatoes that have not ripened in the sun. The extra virgin olive oil will impart a wonderful flavour to the sauce.

Makes 400ml (14fl oz)

extra virgin olive oil

450g (1lb) tomatoes, chopped

about 1 tablespoon tomato purée

salt and freshly ground black pepper

Pour enough olive oil into a frying pan to make a thin film over the base and heat until it is very hot – a haze should rise from it. Add the chopped tomatoes and let them sizzle for a few minutes, then fry gently until they are soft.

Add 1 tablespoon of tomato purée if the tomatoes are very

red and full of flavour, more if they are not fully ripe. Season with salt and pepper, then pass through a food mill.

Parmesan cheese

Parmesan is cow's milk cheese that has been made in the same way for hundreds of years in the Emilia-Romagna region of Italy. It is essential in Italian cooking, imparting a special flavour to dishes. You will notice that we always specify freshly grated Parmesan cheese. Buy a large piece of Parmesan. It will not deteriorate rapidly if kept properly. Cut it up into smallish pieces, then wrap them in 2–3 thicknesses of foil. It will keep well on a low shelf in the refrigerator. Never buy already grated cheese. Parmesan cheese that has been previously grated loses some of its flavour and goes rancid quite quickly.

An electric cheese grater can be bought in Italy, making the job of grating very easy. Less cheese is wasted, as it will grate very close to the hard rind. Look out for one on a trip to Italy (perhaps someone will start to export them now that we use more Parmesan?). Otherwise, a Microplane grater is brilliant.

Béchamel Sauce

Makes 850ml (1½ pints)

700ml (1¼ pints) milk

50g (2oz) butter

2 tablespoons plain flour

salt and freshly ground black pepper

pinch of freshly grated nutmeg

Heat the milk in a saucepan to just below boiling point, then remove the pan from the heat.

Melt the butter in another saucepan, then add the flour and stir well. Add the milk, a little at a time, stirring constantly. Season with salt, pepper and nutmeg.

Cook the sauce for 15 minutes, whisking occasionally with a balloon whisk to ensure a creamy texture.

Salsicce di Maiale Marchigiani

Marchigiani Pork Sausages

Sausage casings are available from good butchers. These sausages will keep for up to 30 days hanging in a refrigerator.

Makes 18–20

1kg (2¼lb) pork shoulder, fat and lean
20g (¾oz) salt
7g (¼oz) coarsely ground black pepper
2 garlic cloves, crushed
pinch of freshly grated nutmeg
pinch of ground allspice
2 tablespoons dry white wine at room temperature, plus extra for soaking sausage casings

Mince the pork, then season with the salt, pepper, garlic and spices. Add the white wine and mix all the ingredients together. Soak the casings in wine for 5 minutes. Using a sausage maker with a standard nozzle, make the sausages. Prick them and hang them in a cool dry place for 3 days before using.

Puff Pastry

225g (8oz) plain flour, sifted, plus extra for dusting
salt
225g (8oz) butter, diced
squeeze of lemon juice
iced water, enough to make a dough

Sift the flour and salt into a bowl, then rub in about a quarter of the butter with your fingertips.

Press the remaining butter firmly in a floured cloth to remove the moisture, then shape into a flat cake.

Add the lemon juice to the flour mixture and mix to a smooth dough with iced water.

The consistency of the dough must be the same as that of the butter.

Knead the dough well and roll it out into a strip a little wider than the butter and rather more than twice its length. Place the butter on one half of the dough, fold the other half over and press the edges together with the rolling pin to form a neat parcel. Leave in a cool place for 15 minutes to allow the butter to harden.

Roll out the dough into a long strip three times the original length but the original width, keeping the corners square and the sides straight to ensure an even thickness when the pastry is folded. Do not let the butter break through the dough. Fold the bottom third up and the top third down, press the edges together with a rolling pin and half-turn the dough so that the folded edges are on the right and left. Roll and fold again and lay aside in a cool place for 15 minutes.

Repeat this process until the dough has been rolled out 6 times. The rolling should be done as evenly as possible and the pastry kept in a long narrow shape which, when folded, forms a square. Roll out as required and leave in a cool place before cooking.

Pasta Frolla

Sweet Pastry

Ingredients may vary according to the pasta dish. Always follow the ingredients for the particular recipe where given, but follow this method for making the pastry.

200g (7oz) plain flour
100g (3½oz) caster sugar
pinch of salt
100g (3½oz) butter, diced
2 egg yolks, beaten
grated rind of 1 lemon

Sift the flour, sugar and salt into a bowl and rub in the butter with your fingertips until the mixture resembles breadcrumbs.

Add the egg yolks and lemon rind. Work the mixture together lightly with your fingertips.

Make into a ball, cover with cling film and leave to rest in the refrigerator for 1 hour.

Shortcrust Pastry

375g (13oz) plain flour
pinch of salt
150g (5oz) butter, diced
warm water, enough to make a dough

Sift the flour and salt into a bowl and rub in the butter with your fingertips until the mixture resembles breadcrumbs.

Add the water, 1–2 tablespoons at a time, and work the mixture together lightly with your fingertips to make a smooth dough.

Shape the dough into a ball, cover with cling film, and leave to rest in the refrigerator for 1 hour.

LASAGNE AND VINCISGRASSI

01

Both lasagne and vincisgrassi are layered and baked pastas. On Ann's first trip to the Marche in the early Sixties she observed that it was the custom for people to take their pasta al forno to the local bakery for baking. Although most houses in the country had outdoor ovens, these would only be lit once or twice a week for a big cooking session. On a daily basis, the bakery was used. After the bread had been cooked, the pasta dishes and meats for roasting went into the ovens. The women would either walk home with their trays of food balanced on a thick folded piece of cloth, on their heads or if they were really lucky, one would see them sitting side-saddle on a Vespa clutching their trays of pasta. That was a sight to be seen. Then suddenly prosperity came and every kitchen sported a brand new cooker.

Lasagne alla bolognese

Lasagne Bolognese

1 quantity Béchamel Sauce
(page 16)

75g (3oz) freshly grated Parmesan
cheese, plus extra for serving

FOR THE PASTA

450g (1lb) Farina O or strong white
plain flour, plus extra for dusting

3 eggs, lightly beaten

175g (6oz) cooked spinach,
well drained and puréed

salt

OR 12–16 sheets ready-made
lasagne verdi

FOR THE RAGÙ BOLOGNESE

4 tablespoons olive oil

75g (3oz) streaky bacon, minced

1 onion, finely chopped

1 carrot, finely chopped

2 celery sticks, finely chopped

350g (12oz) lean minced beef

150ml (¼ pint) dry white wine

300ml (½ pint) water

3 tablespoons tomato purée

2 fresh parsley sprigs, chopped

1 bay leaf

salt and freshly ground
black pepper

serves 4

A fourteenth-century codex, discovered in the University of Bologna, gives a recipe for lasagne more or less as it is made today. We bought some of the very best lasagne on Bologna station many years ago. As the trains drew in, local women would be waiting with huge baskets containing different, piping hot dishes. There was never a bad one. The pasta for lasagne can be either plain – *al uovo* – or coloured green by adding spinach to the basic pasta dough.

To make the pasta, pour the flour into a mixing bowl and make a well in the centre. Pour the eggs into the well and add the spinach and a pinch of salt. Gradually mix into the flour. Work lightly into a rough ball and knead on a floured board for a few minutes until the dough is smooth, shiny and elastic. Wrap in greaseproof paper and leave to rest for 30 minutes. **If making pasta by hand**, divide the dough into four balls and roll out each one lengthways, keeping the surface well floured. Continue until the pasta is paper-thin, then cut into wide strips. **If using a hand pasta machine**, the final thickness should be number 1 setting. Have ready a large saucepan of boiling water. Place the lasagne in the boiling water and when it rises to the top – about 2 minutes – drain and drop into cold water, then drain again and spread out flat on clean tea towels.

To make the ragù, heat the olive oil in a large pan and fry the bacon for 2–3 minutes. Add the onion, carrot and celery and fry for about 5 minutes until they have browned slightly. Add the beef and fry for 5 minutes to seal. Add the wine, water, tomato purée, parsley, bay leaf and seasoning. Lower the heat, cover the pan and simmer for 30–40 minutes. Meanwhile, preheat the oven to 190°C/375°F/gas mark 5. **Make the béchamel sauce** using the method on page 16.

To assemble the lasagne, spread a layer of ragù in the base of a rectangular, earthenware or stainless steel gratin dish, measuring about 30 x 20 x 7.5cm (12 x 8 x 3in). Cover with a layer of béchamel sauce. Sprinkle with Parmesan and cover with pasta. Continue making layers in this way until the dish is full, finishing with a layer of béchamel sauce, sprinkled with a generous topping of Parmesan cheese. Bake the lasagne for about 30 minutes. Remove the dish from the oven and leave to rest for a few minutes before serving with extra Parmesan.

Lasagne con Salsicce

Lasagne with sausage

1¾ quantities Basic Pasta Dough (page 10) OR 12–15 sheets ready-made lasagne

butter, for greasing

FOR THE BÉCHAMEL SAUCE

75g (3oz) butter

75g (3oz) flour

785ml (1¾ pints) milk, warmed

salt

FOR THE SAUCE

10g (½oz) dried porcini mushrooms

4 tablespoons extra virgin olive oil

75g (3oz) onion, finely chopped

315g (11oz) Salsicce di Maiale Marchigiani (page 17) or Continental sausages

400ml (14fl oz) fresh Passata (page 15), or shop-bought

1 clove

salt and freshly ground black pepper

200g (7oz) button mushrooms, sliced

a few drops lemon juice

150g (5oz) mozzarella cheese, sliced

40g (1½ oz) freshly grated Parmesan cheese

serves 6–8

To make the sauce, soak the dried porcini mushrooms in tepid water for 30 minutes. Meanwhile, heat 2 tablespoons of the olive oil in a pan and fry the onion for 3–5 minutes until softened. Add the whole sausages and fry them on all sides.

Add the passata and the clove and season with salt and pepper.

Drain and chop the porcini mushrooms, add to the sauce, cover and cook over a moderate heat, stirring occasionally, for 40 minutes.

Heat the remaining olive oil in a separate pan and quickly fry the button mushrooms, then season with salt, pepper and a few drops of lemon juice. Stir them into the sausage sauce. Preheat the oven to 200°C/400°F/gas mark 6.

Make the béchamel sauce using the method on page 16.

Bring a large saucepan of lightly salted water to the boil and cook the pasta until al dente – about 2 minutes. Drain, drop into cold water, and drain again on clean tea towels. Remove the sausages from the sauce, skin them and cut into slices. Reserve 10 slices of sausage and a ladleful of the mushroom sauce for the topping.

To assemble the lasagne, butter a 30 x 20 x 7.5cm (12 x 8 x 3in) lasagne dish and arrange a layer of pasta over the base, overhanging the sides of the dish. Cover with a little béchamel sauce, then add another layer of pasta, some of the mushroom sauce, some slices of sausage, some mozzarella and a generous sprinkling of grated Parmesan. Continue to make layers, finishing with pasta, then fold the overhanging pasta over the top. Cover the pasta with the reserved sauce and slices of sausage and a generous sprinkling of Parmesan. Bake the lasagne in the oven for 30 minutes. Remove the dish from the oven and leave to rest for a few minutes before serving.

Lasagne di magro

Lenten lasagne

This is a Lenten dish, which is not as rich as the Timpano (page 65). Franco particularly likes fish recipes because fish is cooked a lot in the Marche. He used to serve this at The Walnut Tree on Good Friday.

To make the filling, stick the onion with the clove and put in a pan with the water and two-thirds of the wine. Add the bay leaf and peppercorns. Bring to the boil, season with salt, and simmer for 10 minutes. Add the prawns, cook for 3 minutes, then remove the prawns, peel them and set aside. Strain the stock and reserve.

Melt half the butter in a pan and fry the sole fillets until sealed. Season with salt and pepper, add the remaining wine and cook for 3–4 minutes. Set aside.

Melt the remaining butter in a pan and cook the sliced mushrooms. Season and set aside.

To make the sauce, melt half the butter in a small pan, add the flour and mix together. Cook, stirring, for a few minutes, but do no allow to colour. Add the reserved prawn stock, a little at a time, whisking constantly with a balloon whisk for 10 minutes. When the sauce is tepid, add the Parmesan and season with salt and pepper.

Preheat the oven to 200°C/400°F/gas mark 6.

To assemble the lasagne, butter a 30 x 20 x 7.5cm (12 x 8 x 3in) lasagne dish. Add some of the sauce, then a layer of pasta. Cover with sole, prawns and mushrooms, with their cooking juices, then with another layer of pasta. Continue making layers in this way until all the ingredients have been used, finishing with a layer of sauce. Dot the surface with knobs of butter.

Bake the lasagne for about 15–20 minutes. Remove from the oven and leave to rest for 5 minutes before serving.

---

1 quantity Basic Pasta Dough (page 10) OR 8–9 sheets ready-made lasagne

FOR THE FILLING

1 medium onion, peeled and left whole

1 clove

500ml (18fl oz) water

125ml (4fl oz) dry white wine

1 bay leaf

1 teaspoon black peppercorns

salt and freshly ground black pepper

315g (11oz) unpeeled raw prawns

315g (11oz) Dover sole fillets

50g (2oz) butter

100g (3½oz) button mushrooms, sliced

FOR THE SAUCE

75g (3oz) butter

40g (1¼oz) plain flour

1½ tablespoons freshly grated Parmesan cheese

prawn stock (see method)

salt and freshly ground black pepper

serves 6–8

Lasagne alla Marinara

Seafood lasagne

Make the pasta (page 10) and roll out into wide sheets. The final setting on the pasta machine should be number 1.

For the fish sauce, dice the monkfish into 1cm (½in) cubes. Heat 1 tablespoon of the olive oil and gently fry the monkfish cubes. Remove from the pan and set aside.

Slice the scallops into 3 across the grain. Add 1 tablespoon of the remaining olive oil to the pan and fry the scallops quickly. Remove from the pan and set aside.

Cook the squid in boiling water for 10 minutes, then drain. Slice it into fairly thin rings and set aside.

If the prawns and Dublin Bay prawns are uncooked, boil them in lightly salted water for 5 minutes, then drain. If the lobster is alive, plunge it into salted boiling water and boil for 5 minutes, then drain. Shell all the shellfish and reserve the shells.

Heat the remaining olive oil in a large saucepan and add the onion, carrot, garlic and celery. Add the reserved shells and fry for 2–3 minutes, then add the tomatoes and fry until soft.

Add the water and bouquet garni, bring to the boil, lower the heat and simmer for 1 hour.

Meanwhile, make a beurre manié by blending the butter with the flour.

Strain the mixture through a chinois (an ultra-fine conical sieve) into a clean pan. Return the sauce to the heat and add the beurre manié, in small pieces at a time, blending well until fully incorporated, then cook for 10 minutes.

Add the tomato purée, season with salt, pepper and chilli pepper flakes, then remove from the heat and set aside to cool. When the sauce has cooled, add the fish and shellfish. Preheat the oven to 190°C/375°F/gas mark 5.

Make the béchamel sauce using the method on page 16.

To assemble the lasagne, spread a layer of the fish sauce in the base of a rectangular gratin dish, about 30 x 20 x 7.5cm (12 x 8 x 3in), and top with a layer of béchamel sauce. Sprinkle with Parmesan and cover with pasta. Continue to make layers in this way until the dish is full, finishing with a layer of béchamel sauce, topped with a generous sprinkling of Parmesan. Bake the lasagne for about 30 minutes. Remove and set aside to rest before serving with extra Parmesan.

FOR THE BÉCHAMEL SAUCE

50g (2oz) tablespoons butter

50g (2oz) flour

1.2 litres (2½ pints) hot milk

salt and pepper to taste

pinch of nutmeg

FOR THE PASTA

700g (1lb 10oz) Farina 0 or strong white plain flour

2 egg yolks

4 eggs

pinch of salt

FOR THE FISH SAUCE

225g (8oz) monkfish fillet

4 tablespoons extra virgin olive oil

225g (8oz) shelled scallops, cleaned

225g (8oz) small squid, cleaned

450g (1lb) unpeeled prawns

450g (1lb) unpeeled Dublin Bay prawns

1 small lobster, weighing about 450g (1lb)

1 onion, finely chopped

1 carrot, finely chopped

2 garlic cloves, finely chopped

2 celery sticks, finely chopped

450g (1lb) tomatoes, chopped

1 litre (1¾pints) water

bouquet garni (fresh thyme, parsley, celery tops and bay leaf tied with string)

2 knobs butter

40g (1½oz) plain flour

1 tablespoon tomato purée

salt and freshly ground black pepper

generous pinch of dried chilli flakes

freshly grated Parmesan cheese, plus extra to serve

serves 6

Lasagne ai funghi

Mushroom lasagne

1¾ quantities Basic Pasta Dough (page 10) OR 12–15 sheets ready-made lasagne

75g (3oz) butter, plus extra for greasing

2 tablespoons extra virgin olive oil

315g (11oz) mixed wild mushrooms, sliced

2 tablespoons finely chopped fresh parsley

salt and freshly ground black pepper

2 tablespoons Cognac

FOR THE BÉCHAMEL SAUCE

25g (1oz) flour

40g (1½oz) butter

400ml (14fl oz) milk

salt and freshly ground black pepper

200g (7oz) fontina cheese, thinly sliced

freshly grated Parmesan cheese

serves 6–8

The Romans made a flat wide pasta called *laganum*, which was the precursor of present-day lasagne. Lasagne, as we know it, originates from Emilia. Although the traditional Emilian lasagne involves layers of the wide pasta strips, which are briefly boiled, with a meat sauce, béchamel and parmesan, there are many varieties that feature fish and vegetables, like this one.

Make the pasta (page 10) and roll out into wide sheets. The final setting on the pasta machine should be number 1.

Make the béchamel sauce using the method on page 16.

Melt half the butter with the olive oil and fry the mushrooms briskly with the chopped parsley. Season with salt and pepper, sprinkle with the Cognac and finish cooking over a moderate heat. Bring a large pan of lightly salted water to the boil. Cook the lasagne, a few sheets at a time, until al dente – about 2 minutes. Drain, drop into cold water, and drain again on clean tea towels. Preheat the oven to 190°C/375°F/gas mark 5.

To assemble the lasagne, generously butter a 30 x 20 x 7.5cm (12 x 8 x 3in) gratin dish. Line the dish with a layer of pasta, slightly overlapping. Add a layer of the mushroom mixture, some béchamel sauce and a few thin slices of fontina. Continue making layers, alternating the pasta layers until all the ingredients have been used. Finish with a layer of mushrooms and béchamel sauce. Smooth the top over, sprinkle with Parmesan and flakes of butter.

Bake for about 30 minutes. Remove from the oven and leave to rest for 5 minutes before cutting and serving.

Ⓥ

Lasagne di Carnevale alla Napoletana

Neapolitan carnival lasagne

This is typical of the pasta dishes eaten during Carnival, the days leading up to Lent. It is a rich, substantial dish and, apart from a salad, no other course is required.

Make the pasta (page 10) and roll out into wide sheets. The final setting on the pasta machine should be number 1

Melt 50g (2oz) of the butter with 125ml (4fl oz) of the olive oil in a large pan and fry the onion, pancetta, carrot and celery. Add the loin of pork in one piece and fry on both sides to seal.

When the vegetables are soft and golden, add the tomato purée and red wine. Season with salt and pepper. Then, as they would say in Naples, *tirare il ragù* – that is, cover and cook the sauce very slowly for about 1 hour. Stir frequently and add a little water when needed.

Meanwhile, heat 2 tablespoons of the remaining olive oil in a frying pan and fry the sausage until cooked through. Remove from the pan, peel off the casing and slice thinly. Set aside. Sieve the ricotta into a bowl, add 1 egg, 4 tablespoons of the Parmesan and a pinch of salt and pepper. Mix together.

When the pork is cooked, remove it from the sauce and chop finely. Return half the meat to the sauce and put the rest in a bowl. Add the remaining egg, 1 tablespoon of the remaining Parmesan and the breadcrumbs to the bowl. Mix all the ingredients together and shape into little balls the size of a large marble. Heat the remaining olive oil in a frying pan and fry the little meatballs until browned all over. Remove from the pan and set aside. Preheat the oven to 180°C/350°F/gas mark 4.

Bring a large saucepan of lightly salted water to the boil and cook the pasta, 3–4 pieces at a time, until al dente – about 2 minutes. Drain, drop into cold water, and drain again on clean tea towels.

To assemble the lasagne, butter a 30 x 20 x 7.5cm (12 x 8 x 3in) lasagne dish with the remaining butter. Place a layer of pasta in the base, followed by a layer of the ricotta mixture, a little of the sauce, a few meatballs, some slices of sausage and some mozzarella. Continue making layers in this way until all the ingredients have been used, sprinkling the last layer of pasta with a generous amount of Parmesan, then covering it with mozzarella and the meat sauce. Bake for about 20 minutes, then serve immediately.

1 quantity Basic Pasta Dough (page 10) OR 8–9 sheets ready-made lasagne

FOR THE SAUCE
100g (3½oz) butter
200ml (7fl oz) extra virgin olive oil
75g (3oz) pancetta, finely chopped
1 onion, finely chopped
1 carrot, finely chopped
1 celery stick, finely chopped
315g (11oz) loin of pork
3–4 tablespoons tomato purée
75ml (3fl oz) red wine
salt and freshly ground black pepper
200g (7oz) Italian sausage

315g (11oz) ricotta cheese
2 eggs
100g (3½oz) freshly grated Parmesan cheese
25g (1oz) fresh breadcrumbs
315g (11oz) mozzarella cheese, thinly sliced

serves 6–8

Lasagne con Sugo d'Anitra

Lasagne with duck sauce

Make the pasta (page 10) and roll out into wide sheets. The final setting on the pasta machine should be number 1.

To make the stock, place all the vegetables in a large saucepan with the herbs and peppercorns. Add cold water to cover. Bring to the boil, lower the heat and simmer for 30–45 minutes. Strain the liquid and reserve. (You should be left with 700ml (1¼ pints) stock.)

To make the duck sauce, joint the duck, discarding as much fat as possible. Reserve the liver, neck and wings. Meanwhile, heat 2 tablespoons of the olive oil in a large frying pan and fry the duck pieces until the skin is crisp. Transfer the duck pieces to a flameproof casserole. Add the neck and wings. Coarsely chop the liver and fry briefly in 1 tablespoon of the remaining olive oil. Remove from the pan and reserve.

Heat the remaining olive oil in another frying pan and fry the pancetta. Add the vegetables and fry until softened. Transfer the vegetable mixture to the casserole. Pour the wine into the frying pan and heat until reduced by half, then add to the casserole with the bay leaves, parsley, lemon peel and tomato purée. Add hot water to cover.

Cover the casserole and cook over a moderate heat for 45 minutes–1 hour. Remove and discard the bay leaves, parsley and lemon peel. Check for tenderness. When ready, remove the meat from the bones and chop coarsely, then return it to the sauce. Add the duck liver and cook for a few minutes. Check the consistency, which should be that of dense ragù. Check the seasoning.

To make the stock-béchamel, melt the butter, then stir in the flour. Cook over a gentle heat, stirring constantly with a wooden spoon, for 3–4 minutes. Pour in the warm vegetable stock and beat well with a balloon whisk. Season with salt.

Preheat the oven to 200°C/400°F/gas mark 6. Bring a large pan of lightly salted water to the boil. Cook the lasagne, a few sheets at a time, until al dente – about 2 minutes. Drain, drop into cold water, and drain again on clean tea towels.

Butter a gratin dish, about 30 x 20 x 7.5cm (12 x 8 x 3in). Place a thin layer of stock-béchamel over the base, followed by a layer of pasta, a layer of duck sauce and another layer of stock-béchamel. Scatter with spinach and sprinkle with Parmesan. Continue making layers in this way, finishing with stock-béchamel, Parmesan and a few leaves of spinach. Bake for 30–40 minutes. Remove from the oven and leave to rest before serving.

1¾ quantities Basic Pasta Dough (page 10) OR 12–15 sheets ready-made lasagne

butter, for greasing

250g (9oz) spinach, lightly cooked

freshly grated Parmesan cheese

FOR THE STOCK

2 onions, coarsely chopped

2 carrots, coarsely chopped

2 celery sticks, coarsely chopped

1 small bunch fresh parsley

4 bay leaves

8 peppercorns

1 litre (1¾ pints) water

FOR THE DUCK SAUCE

2kg (4½lb) duck

5 tablespoons extra virgin olive oil

75g (3oz) pancetta, finely chopped

150g (5oz) onion, finely chopped

1 small carrot, finely chopped

1 celery stick, finely chopped

75ml (3fl oz) dry white wine

3 bay leaves

fresh parsley

3 strips lemon peel

150g (5oz) tomato purée

FOR THE STOCK-BÉCHAMEL

60g (2½oz) butter

60g (2½oz) flour

700ml (1¼ pints) warm vegetable stock

salt

serves 8–10

Lasagne agli Asparagi

Lasagne with Asparagus

1½ quantities Basic Pasta Dough (page 10) OR 12 sheets ready-made lasagne

knob of butter, plus extra for greasing and finishing

500g (18oz) short asparagus or standard lengths cut into 3 pieces, cooked until al dente

3 basil leaves, torn

220ml (7¾fl oz) single cream

40g (1½oz) Emmenthal cheese, freshly grated

FOR THE BÉCHAMEL SAUCE

500ml (18fl oz) milk

50g (2oz) butter

50g (2oz) flour

salt and freshly ground black pepper

serves 6–8

Make the pasta (page 10) and roll out into wide sheets. The final setting on the pasta machine should be number 1.

Bring a large pan of lightly salted water to the boil. Cook the pasta a few sheets at a time, until al dente – about 2 minutes. Drain, drop into cold water and drain again on clean tea towels.

To make the béchamel sauce, heat the milk in a saucepan to just below boiling point, then remove the pan from the heat.

Melt the butter in another saucepan, then add the flour and stir well. Add the milk, a little at a time, stirring constantly. Cook the sauce for 15 minutes, whisking occasionally with a balloon whisk to ensure a creamy texture.

Season the sauce with salt and pepper and stir in the grated Emmenthal.

Fold in the asparagus, basil leaves, a knob of butter and the cream.

Preheat the oven to 190°C/375°C/gas mark 5.

To assemble the lasagne, butter a 30 x 20 x 7.5cm (12 x 8 x 3in) gratin dish. Cover the base with a layer of pasta, then a layer of asparagus sauce. Continue making layers in this way until all the ingredients have been used. Dot the last layer of pasta with butter.

Bake the lasagne for 45–50 minutes. Serve.

Ⓥ

Lasagne alla Calabrese

Calabrian lasagne

Skin and break up the sausages. Heat the oil in a frying pan, briefly fry the garlic, then add the crumbled sausages and fry for 3–4 minutes. Add the tomatoes, tomato purée mixture, basil, salt and pepper. Add a little water if the mixture seems too thick. Simmer the sauce until it is fairly thick.

Bring a large pan of lightly salted water to the boil. Cook the lasagne, a few sheets at a time, until al dente – about 2 minutes. Drain, drop into cold water, and drain again on clean tea towels. Preheat the oven to 200°C/400°F/gas mark 6.

To assemble the lasagne, oil a 30 x 20 x 7.5cm (12 x 8 x 3in) lasagne dish. Place a layer of pasta in the base, then add a layer of ricotta and a few slices of mozzarella. Follow this with a layer of mushrooms, then a layer of sausage sauce. Continue making layers in this way, finishing with a layer of sausage sauce and a layer of freshly grated Parmesan.

Bake the pasta in the oven for 30–40 minutes. Remove from the oven and leave to rest for 5 minutes before cutting and serving.

450g (1lb) dried lasagne or 700g (1½lb) fresh lasagne

125g (4½oz) Italian pork sausage

125g (4½oz) spicy Italian sausage

2 garlic cloves, finely chopped

4 tablespoons extra virgin olive oil, plus extra for greasing

200g (7oz) plum tomatoes, peeled, seeded and sliced

4 tablespoons tomato purée mixed with 4 tablespoons water

12 basil leaves, finely torn

salt and freshly ground black pepper

500g (18oz) ricotta, crumbled

200g (7oz) mozzarella cheese, thinly sliced

375g (13oz) mushrooms, sliced and cooked in a little olive oil

50g (2oz) freshly grated Parmesan cheese

serves 8–10

Vincisgrassi

75g (3oz) butter, plus extra for greasing

150g (5oz) freshly grated Parmesan cheese, plus extra to serve (optional)

truffle oil, or, if possible, a little shaved white truffle

FOR THE PASTA

500g (18oz) Farina 0 or strong plain white flour, plus extra for dusting

2 eggs

4 egg yolks

1 teaspoon salt

FOR THE SAUCE

1.2 litres (2 pints) milk

50g (2oz) butter

50g (2oz) plain flour

4 tablespoons extra virgin olive oil

400g (14oz) porcini mushrooms, sliced

200g (7oz) Parma ham, cut into julienne strips

200ml (7fl oz) single cream

3 tablespoons finely chopped fresh parsley

salt and freshly ground black pepper

serves 6

The story goes that vincisgrassi was named after an Austrian general Windisch Graets, who was with his troops in Ancona in 1799 during the Napoleonic War. Actually Antonio Nebbia, who wrote a gastronomic manual in 1784, mentioned in his book a similar dish called *princisgras*. For this recipe, formerly a signature dish of The Walnut Tree Inn, we collect porcini from the woods around Abergavenny.

Make a dough from the ingredients listed, knead well and roll through a pasta machine as you would for lasagne (page 10). Cut the pasta lengths into 12.5cm (5in) squares.

Bring a large pan of lightly salted water to the boil. Cook the lasagne, a few squares at a time, until al dente – about 2 minutes. Drain, drop into cold water, and drain again on clean tea towels.

To make the sauce, heat the milk in a saucepan to just below boiling point, then remove the pan from the heat.

Melt the butter in another saucepan, add the flour and mix well. Add the milk, a little at a time, beating well with a balloon whisk. Cook for 15 minutes, stirring occasionally with a balloon whisk.

Meanwhile, heat the oil in a large frying pan and cook the porcini until tender. Add them to the sauce and stir in the Parma ham, cream and parsley. Season with salt and pepper and bring to the boil. Turn off the heat.

Preheat the oven to 220°C/425°F/gas mark 7.

To assemble the vincisgrassi, butter a 30 x 20 x 7.5cm (12 x 8 x 3in) gratin dish and cover the base with a layer of pasta. Spread a layer of the sauce on top, dot with butter and sprinkle with some Parmesan. Continue making layers in the same way, finishing with a layer of sauce and a sprinkling of Parmesan.

Bake for 20 minutes. Serve with a little truffle oil splashed on top or, better still, with shavings of white truffle, and a little extra Parmesan.

Lasagne al Pesto e Porcini

Lasagne with Pesto and Fresh Porcini Mushrooms

1½ quantities Basic Pasta Dough
(page 10) OR 12 sheets ready-
made lasagne

butter, for greasing

freshly grated Parmesan cheese

FOR THE BÉCHAMEL SAUCE

40g (1½oz) butter

40g (1½oz) flour

500ml (18fl oz) milk

salt and freshly ground black
pepper

pinch of freshly grated nutmeg

FOR THE MUSHROOMS

500g (18oz) porcini mushrooms

40g (1½oz) butter

1 garlic clove, finely chopped

FOR THE PESTO

25 large fresh basil leaves

1 garlic clove

50g (2oz) pine nuts

50g (2oz) freshly grated pecorino
cheese

150ml (¼ pint) extra virgin olive oil

serves 6

'The soul of pesto may be basil, but its heart is garlic'. This is a modern recipe – in the sense of less than 50 years old – from the region of Liguria.

Make the pasta (page 10) and roll out into wide sheets. The final setting on the pasta machine should be number 1. Bring a large pan of lightly salted water to the boil. Cook the lasagne, a few sheets at a time, until al dente – about 2 minutes. Drain, drop into cold water, and drain again on clean tea towels.

Clean the porcini mushrooms thoroughly, brushing off any dirt with a soft brush, then slice them. Melt the butter in a large pan and fry the mushrooms with the garlic for about 10 minutes. Remove from the pan and set aside.

Make the béchamel sauce using the method on page 16.

To make the pesto, place the basil, garlic, pine nuts and pecorino in a blender and blend for a few seconds. Then, with the motor running, gradually add the oil, pouring it in very slowly until the sauce has a fluid consistency.

Preheat the oven to 200°C/400°F/gas mark 6.

To assemble the lasagne, butter a rectangular gratin dish, about 30 x 20 x 7.5cm (12 x 8 x 3in). Put a layer of pasta on the base, then cover with a layer of pesto, followed by a layer of pasta again, then a layer of porcini with a little béchamel sauce. Continue making layers in this way until all the ingredients have been used. Finish with a layer of porcini and béchamel sauce and sprinkle with the Parmesan.

Bake the lasagne for about 30–40 minutes or until the top is golden brown.

Remove from the oven and leave to rest for 5 minutes before serving.

Ⓥ

Vincisgrassi con Carne

Vincisgrassi with Meat

Among the many *sagras* (festivals) that occur during the summer months of July to September in the Marche region, there is one dedicated to vincisgrassi. It is held on a Sunday in July in Cartoceto, a small village of four hundred people in the province of Pesaro. Four to five thousand people gather together to have a plate of Vincisgrassi con Carne and drink local wine.

Make a dough from the ingredients listed, knead well and roll through the pasta machine as you would for lasagne (page 10). Cut the dough into 12.5cm (5in) squares.

Bring a large pan of lightly salted water to the boil. Cook the lasagne, a few sheets at a time, until al dente – about 2 minutes. Drain, drop into cold water, and drain again on clean tea towels.

To make the meat sauce, heat the oil in a large pan and fry the bacon. Add the garlic, onion, celery and carrot and fry until lightly golden. Add the minced beef, breaking it up with a fork and cook until sealed.

Pour in the wine and allow to bubble away. Add hot water to cover, then add the tomato purée, bay leaf and cloves. Season with salt and pepper. Lower the heat and simmer for about 2 hours until tender. (This will vary depending on the cut of meat used.)

Add the chicken livers and cook briefly. Taste and adjust the seasoning if necessary.

Preheat the oven to 190°C/375F/gas mark 5.

To assemble the vincisgrassi, lightly oil a 30 x 20 x 7.5cm (12 x 8 x 3in) gratin dish. Place a layer of pasta in the base, cover with a layer of Parmesan and then add a layer of meat sauce. Continue making layers in this way until all the ingredients are used, finishing with a layer of pasta. Sprinkle with Parmesan and dot with the butter.

Bake the vincisgrassi in the oven until the top is browned, then serve with extra Parmesan.

freshly grated Parmesan cheese
25g (1oz) butter, diced

FOR THE PASTA
500g (18oz) Farina 0 or strong plain white flour, plus extra for dusting
2 eggs
4 egg yolks
1 teaspoon salt

FOR THE MEAT SAUCE
4 tablespoons olive oil, plus extra for greasing
100g (3½oz) streaky bacon, minced
2 garlic cloves, finely chopped
1 onion, finely chopped
1 celery stick, finely chopped
1 carrot, finely chopped
450g (1lb) lean minced beef
175ml (6fl oz') dry white wine
250ml (9fl oz) tomato purée
1 bay leaf
4 cloves
salt and freshly ground black pepper
175g (6oz) chicken livers, finely chopped

serves 4–6

TIMBALLI AND PASTICCI

02

A timballo is a moulded pasta dish with a pastry crust. The word timballo derives from *tambouro*, a tambourine which comes from the Arab-Persian word *atabal*. The silver container that this dish was cooked in resembles a tambourine. In Sicilian dialect, a timballo is known as a *sfumatu* or a *timmala*. Timballi arrived in Sicily from Arabia in the ninth century. During the Renaissance period, timballi were always served at major banquets and even today ,they are eaten on important occasions. The preparation of these dishes may take time, but they are well worth it.

Generally speaking, a pasticcio is a rich, elaborate composition of short stubby pasta with a meat sauce, truffles or mushrooms, layered with a béchamel sauce and cheese. It can be less elaborate, but like the timballo, it is a dish prepared for festive occasions. It is very substantial and is eaten as a main course. Pasticci are among the oldest kind of pasta dishes.

Pasta 'ncasciata

Pasta in an Aubergine Case

500g (18oz) aubergines

315g (11oz) finely minced pork

4 eggs, optional

75g (3oz) freshly grated pecorino

4 tablespoons finely chopped parsley

salt and freshly ground black pepper

1kg (2¼lb) ripe plum tomatoes, peeled, seeded and diced

40g (1½oz) tomato purée, mixed with 1–2 tablespoons water

2 garlic cloves, finely chopped

125ml (4fl oz) extra virgin olive oil

20–25 fresh basil leaves, torn

100g (3½oz) spicy sausages, skinned and crumbled

500g (18oz) mezze zite or penne

110g (4oz) dried breadcrumbs

200g (7oz) *mozzarella di bufala*

100g (3½oz) caciocavallo cheese, thinly sliced

serves 6–8

Pasta 'ncasciata is a rich and typically Baroque dish found in Messina and Ragusa in Sicily. It is an impressive dish for important occasions, especially weddings. In dialect, *'ncasciata* means *incassata, sistemata in cassa* – 'in a case'. The hard-boiled eggs can be omitted if you prefer.

Thinly slice the aubergines lengthways and place in a colander. Sprinkle with salt and set aside for 30 minutes to drain.

Mix the minced pork with 1 egg, half the pecorino and the chopped parsley in a bowl. Season with salt and pepper.

Dampen your fingers with cold water and shape the mixture into little balls, the size of a cherry. Make sure the surface of the balls is smooth.

Put the tomatoes, diluted tomato purée and garlic into a heavy, flameproof casserole with some of the extra virgin olive oil. Heat gently until the mixture boils, then add the basil and meatballs and season lightly. Cook the sauce for 15 minutes, occasionally stirring gently so that the meatballs do not break up.

Add the sausage meat, and cook for a further 30 minutes or until the sauce is thick. Check the seasoning.

Meanwhile, hard-boil the remaining eggs, then shell and slice.

Pat dry the aubergine slices on kitchen paper. Heat some of the remaining oil in a frying pan and fry the slices until golden on both sides, or griddle (the healthier option!).

Bring a large saucepan of lightly salted water to the boil and cook the pasta until just under al dente. Drain and turn into a large bowl. Pour over the tomato, meatball and sausage sauce. Add the remaining pecorino and mix well, taking care not to break up the meatballs or sausage meat.

Preheat the oven to 200°C/400°F/gas mark 6.

Oil a 26cm (10½in) diameter spring-clip tin and sprinkle with breadcrumbs. Line the tin with the aubergine slices, spoon a layer of half the pasta and sauce into the tin and some slices of egg, mozzarella and caciocavallo. Add the remaining pasta, then the remaining egg, mozzarella and caciocavallo. Cover with the remaining aubergines and bake for 30–35 minutes.

Timballu a Gattupardu

Timballo Gattopardo

350g (12oz) maltagliati

40g (1½oz) freshly grated Parmesan cheese

beaten egg yolk, for brushing

FOR THE PASTA FROLLA

400g (14oz) plain flour, plus extra for dusting

200g (7oz) sugar

pinch of salt

200g (7oz) butter, plus extra for greasing

2 eggs and an extra egg yolk

FOR THE SAUCE

3 tablespoons extra virgin olive oil

100g (3½oz) finely chopped onion

½ carrot, finely chopped

1 celery stick, finely chopped

50g (2oz) Parma ham, cut into julienne strips

100g (3½oz) skinless, boneless chicken breast, thinly sliced

150g (5oz) chicken livers, cleaned and thinly sliced

100g (3½oz) porcini mushrooms, thinly sliced

salt and freshly ground black pepper

pinch of ground cinnamon

75g (3oz) skinned and slivered pistachio nuts

150ml (¼ pint) Marsala

1 teaspoon cornflour

FOR THE BÉCHAMEL SAUCE

500ml (18fl oz) milk

40g (1½oz) butter

40g (1½oz) flour

salt and freshly ground black pepper

serves 6–8

This dish was temptingly described by Guiseppe di Lampedusa in his book *Il Gattopardo* (The Leopard):

'The burnished gold of the crusts, the fragrance of sugar and cinnamon they exuded, were but preludes to the delights released from the interior when the knife broke the crust; first came a spice-laden haze, then chicken livers, hard-boiled eggs, sliced ham, chicken and truffles in masses of piping hot, glistening macaroni, to which the great meat juice gave an exquisite hue of suede.'

Make the pasta frolla (page 18), then leave to rest, covered with a cloth, for 1 hour in the refrigerator.

Butter a 23cm (9 inch) deep, circular springform tin. Cut off two-thirds of the pastry and roll it out into a circle 5mm (¼in) thick. Line the tin with the pastry. Make another circle with the remaining dough, for a lid, and reserve.

To make the sauce, heat the oil in a frying pan and cook the onion, carrot and celery until soft and golden. Add the Parma ham and chicken breast, fry for 1–2 minutes, then add the chicken livers and mushrooms. Season with salt, pepper and cinnamon. Stir in the pistachio slivers. Add the Marsala and reduce over low heat.

Mix the cornflour with a little cold water to a smooth paste, stir it into the sauce and cook until thickened.

Preheat the oven to 200°C/400°F/gas mark 6.

Make the béchamel sauce using the method on page 16.

Meanwhile, bring a large saucepan of lightly salted water to the boil and cook the maltagliati to just under al dente. Add the pasta to the sauce, then add the béchamel and Parmesan, mix well and pour the mixture into the pastry-lined tin. Cover with the remaining circle of dough and seal the edges. Decorate the top and brush with beaten egg yolk. Prick the lid with a fork. Bake for 35–40 minutes. Remove from the oven and leave the pie to rest for 10 minutes before serving.

Timballo di Maccheroni Napoletana

Neapolitan Timballo of Maccheroni

During the seventeenth and eighteen centuries, Naples was one of the richest courts in Europe, and the Neopolitans were renowned for their lavish banquets.

Place the dried mushrooms in a bowl, add cold water to cover and allow to soak for 30 minutes.

Meanwhile, make the pastry (page 18). Butter a 24cm (9½in) loose-based cake tin. Cut off two-thirds of the pastry and roll out on a lightly floured surface, then use to line the tin. Chill in the refrigerator until required. Form the remaining pastry into a ball, wrap in foil and chill in the refrigerator until required.

Melt half the butter in a frying pan and cook the onions over a low heat until soft. Add the peas and water and cook until the peas are tender and the water has evaporated. Remove the pan from the heat, season with salt and set aside to cool.

Drain the mushrooms, pat dry with kitchen paper and chop finely. Melt the remaining butter in a frying pan and cook the mushrooms for 2 minutes, add the wine and remove from the heat. Stir in the 2 tablespoons water and set aside to cool.

To make the salsa napolitana, heat the oil in a medium saucepan. Add the tomatoes, garlic and salt to taste and cook over a low heat for 15 minutes. Remove from the heat, stir in the sugar and set aside to cool.

Bring a large saucepan of lightly salted water to the boil and cook the maltagliati until al dente. Drain, turn into a large bowl, sprinkle over the Parmesan and Gruyère, and toss well.

Preheat the oven to 230°C/450°F/gas mark 8.

Toss the cold pasta with a little cold tomato sauce. Put half the pasta in the pastry case, cover with half the tomato sauce followed by half the mushroom sauce, half the onion and pea mixture and half the diced mozzarella. Repeat the process.

Roll out the remaining pastry to make a lid for the pie. Cover the pie with the lid and seal well. Brush the lid with beaten egg yolk and prick the centre.

Bake for 10 minutes, then reduce the oven temperature to 200°C/400°F/gas mark 6 and bake for a further 30 minutes.

Remove the pie from the oven and leave to rest for 10 minutes before serving.

50g (2oz) dried porcini mushrooms

75g (3oz) butter

200g (7oz) onions, finely chopped

315g (11oz) peas, fresh or frozen

175ml (6fl oz) water

salt

100ml (3½fl oz) white wine

500g (18oz) dried maltagliati

75g (3oz) Parmesan cheese, freshly grated

75g (3oz) Gruyère cheese, grated

315g (11oz) mozzarella, diced

1 egg yolk, beaten, for brushing

FOR THE PASTRY

500g (18oz) plain white flour, plus extra for dusting

pinch of salt

250g (9oz) butter, plus extra for greasing

2 eggs

100ml (3½fl oz) water

FOR THE SALSA NAPOLITANA

4 tablespoons extra virgin olive oil

800g (1¾lb) tomatoes, peeled, seeded and coarsely chopped

3 garlic cloves, finely chopped

salt

1 teaspoon sugar

serves 10

Truffles...

White truffles are always used raw as a condiment and are best on bland dishes; they dissolve in the mouth. We have had a few funny experiences with white truffles. Once, on a fleeting visit to Italy, Franco could not resist purchasing a few kilos of white truffles. He asked the *tartufaio* to wrap them in newspaper and then seal them well in a polysterene box. Despite its being winter, it was a hot afternoon. When we arrived at Bologna Airport, our luggage, with the truffles buried inside, was checked through. We showed our documents for the truffles to the customs officer on duty and through we went to the departure lounge. The intended time of our departure came and went. I heard two *carabinieri* mention my husband's name – he was fast asleep. Suddenly, there was an announcement over the tannoy: 'Signor Franco Taruschio per favore.' Quickly I awakened Franco. Two big burly *carabinieri* came towards him, machine guns slung over their shoulders, and marched him off. He was taken to a hangar where his suitcase stood in the middle. No one spoke. Three more *carabinieri* joined them with dogs straining on their leads. One of the men turned to Franco and said, 'We believe you have some kind of gas in your suitcase'.

Franco laughed, 'No, no, it's truffles'.

'Open your suitcase then.'

As Franco bent down to open his case, he heard the guns being cocked. He prayed that their fingers wouldn't slip. Frantically, he opened the box and the truffles tumbled out. There was relieved laughter all round. The dogs sent into the hold of the plane to check for bombs or drugs had smelt the truffles and gone crazy. No wonder they use dogs in Italy to scent out the prized truffle. The Marche is also famed for *tartufo nero pregiato*, the Perigord-type truffle and the less precious variety of *tartufo nero scorzone*, the summer truffle. The black truffle is entirely different from the white truffle: it has a herbaceous and spicy flavour and a chewy texture. The black truffle is cooked to bring out its aroma which complements many dishes.

We have always bought our truffles from St Angelo in Vado, a small town situated in the Pesarese Appenines, a mountainous chain with three valleys, each with a river flowing down to the Adriatic sea. A local legend has it that in 1668, Cardinal Cesare Rasponi, when resident in Urbino, an ancient university town near St Angelo, sent a gift of two truffles to his cousin Cardinal Flavio Chigi, nephew of Pope Alessandro VII. These truffles weighed 18kg (39½lb) and 34kg (75lb) respectively. They were supposed to have been found on the estate of Filippo Cortese da Bologna. So for centuries, this area has been known for its abundance of truffles.

Timballo di Bonifacio VIII

Bonifacio's Timballo

Pope Bonifacio VIII lived in Anagni Lazio. This pope was insulted by the emissary of Filipo il Bello in 1303. The episode was known as the Slap of Anagni and was made famous by Dante in the *CXX Canto of Purgatory*. Bonifacio seems nowadays to be remembered more for this dish; a speciality of Anagni.

Cover the pastry with a cloth and leave in the refrigerator to rest for 2 hours.

To make the meatballs, combine the minced beef, parsley, pancetta, egg, pecorino and breadcrumbs, season with salt and pepper and mix together thoroughly.

Dampen your hands and roll small pieces of the mixture into cherry-size meatballs. Set aside.

To make the sauce, heat the oil in a frying pan and cook the onion, carrot, celery and pancetta until the vegetables are soft.

Add the chicken livers and mushrooms and cook for 1–2 minutes, turning the livers over. Add the wine and cook until it has evaporated.

Add the passata, season with salt and pepper, cover and cook, over a low heat for 40 minutes. Add the meatballs to the sauce, re-cover and cook for a further 20 minutes.

Meanwhile, bring a large saucepan of lightly salted water to the boil and cook the pasta until very al dente. Drain, turn into a large bowl and toss with a generous ladle of the tomato and meatball sauce. Set aside to cool.

Preheat the oven to 190°C/375°F/gas mark 5.

Cut off two-thirds of the pastry, roll out on a lightly floured surface and line a 26cm (10¼in) round, springform tin. Cover the pastry with slices of Parma ham, allowing it to overhang the edge. Cover with a layer of pasta, followed by a layer of meatball sauce and a sprinkling of Parmesan. Continue making layers in this way until all the ingredients have been used. If using truffles, shave them between the layers. Fold in the overhanging ham.

Roll out the remaining pastry to make a lid. Place it over the top of the pie and seal well. Bake for 40–50 minutes. Remove the pie from the oven and leave to stand for 5 minutes, then remove from the tin and serve, cut into wedges.

salt

315g (11oz) zite or maccaroni ciociara (very fine noodles), or tagliolini

1 quantity Shortcrust Pastry (see page 18) plain flour, for dusting

200g (7oz) Parma ham, sliced

4 tablespoons freshly grated Parmesan cheese

black or white truffles (optional)

FOR THE MEATBALLS

315g (11oz) minced beef

1 bunch of fresh parsley, finely chopped

25g (1oz) pancetta, finely chopped

1 egg

1 tablespoon freshly grated pecorino cheese

1 tablespoon fresh breadcrumbs

salt and freshly ground black pepper

FOR THE SAUCE

4 tablespoons extra virgin olive oil

1 small onion, finely chopped

1 carrot, finely chopped

1 celery stick, finely chopped

25g (1oz) pancetta, finely chopped

100g (3½oz) chicken livers, cleaned and chopped

25g (1oz) dried porcini mushrooms, soaked in lukewarm water for 30 minutes, drained and sliced

175ml (6fl oz) red wine

500ml (18fl oz) fresh Passata (page 15) or shop-bought

salt and freshly ground black pepper

serves 8–10

Timballo di Vermicelli con Pesce per la Domenica delle Palme

salt

450g (1lb) vermicelli

FOR THE PASTRY

450g (1lb) plain flour, plus extra for dusting

1 teaspoon salt

225g (8oz) butter

2 eggs, beaten

FOR THE FISH BALLS

450g (1lb) cod or other white fish fillet, skinned

100g (3½oz) black olives, stoned

1 tablespoon salted capers, well rinsed

1 tablespoon pine nuts

4 tablespoons finely chopped fresh parsley

salt and freshly ground black pepper

2 tablespoons extra virgin olive oil, plus extra for frying

10 tablespoons fresh breadcrumbs

FOR THE SEAFOOD SAUCE

3 tablespoons extra virgin olive oil

700g (1½lb) plum tomatoes, peeled, seeded and diced

1 tablespoon tomato purée (optional)

175g (6oz) shelled peas, blanched

175g (6oz) button mushrooms, sliced and fried in a little olive oil

450g (1lb) mixed cooked shelled seafood (mussels, Venus and other clams, prawns)

salt and freshly ground black pepper

FOR THE ANCHOVY SAUCE

3 tablespoons extra virgin olive oil

1 garlic clove, crushed

10 salt-cured anchovy fillets, well rinsed

4 tablespoons finely chopped fresh parsley

freshly ground black pepper

serves 6–8

Palm Sunday Timballo of Vermicelli and Fish

Make the pastry (page 18). Cut off one-third of the pastry, shape into a ball, wrap in foil and reserve in the refrigerator. Roll out the larger piece of dough to a circle large enough to line a 26cm (10¼in) loose-based tin. Line the tin and chill in the refrigerator until required.

To make the fish balls, dice the fish and place in a food processor with the olives, capers, pine nuts and parsley. Season with salt and pepper and process to make a firm paste. Add the olive oil to soften, then add 2 tablespoons of the breadcrumbs to bind well together. Scrape the mixture into a bowl. Spread out the remaining breadcrumbs on a flat plate. Heat the olive oil for frying.

Dampen your hands and shape small pieces of the fish mixture into balls the size of a cherry tomato. Roll the fish balls in the breadcrumbs and fry in the olive oil until golden. Drain on kitchen paper.

To make the seafood sauce, heat the olive oil in a large saucepan and fry the tomatoes gently until they have disintegrated. If the tomatoes are not very ripe, add the tomato purée.

Remove the pan from the heat and add the peas, mushrooms and mixed seafood. Season with salt and pepper and set aside. .

Bring a large saucepan of salted water to the boil and cook the vermicelli until al dente. Drain.

Meanwhile, make the anchovy sauce. Heat the olive oil in a frying pan then add the garlic followed by the anchovy fillets and parsley. Season with a generous amount of pepper. Cook until the anchovy fillets have broken down. Drain the pasta and toss in the anchovy sauce.

Preheat the oven to 200°C/400°F/gas mark 6.

Roll out the reserved pastry to make a lid large enough to fit the pastry-line tin.

Put a layer of pasta into the pastry case, scatter over some fish balls, then spoon over a layer of seafood sauce. Continue making layers in this way, finishing with a layer of pasta.Cover with the pastry lid and bake for 45 minutes.Remove the pie from the oven and leave to stand for 5 minutes. Remove from the tin and serve cut into wedges.

Timballo di Pasta al Forno Eoliana

Timballo of Tagliatelle with Ricotta and Capers

4 tablespoons extra virgin olive oil

1 small onion, finely chopped

1 garlic clove, finely chopped

600g (1¼lb) plum tomatoes, peeled, seeded and chopped

4 salted anchovy fillets, well rinsed

4 tablespoons salted capers, well rinsed

10–15 fresh basil leaves, torn

salt and freshly ground black pepper

315g (11oz) ricotta cheese, sieved

25g (1oz) freshly grated Parmesan cheese

25g (1oz) freshly grated pecorino cheese

400g (14oz) fresh tagliatelle

butter, for greasing

225g (8oz) mozzarella cheese, sliced

serves 4–6

The Eolian islands are famous for their capers and the locals use them in as many dishes as they can. The bushes grow on rocky terrain or even in dry walls and have small, delicate, orchid-like flowers. These are rarely seen, as the capers – flower buds – are picked before the bushes have a chance to blossom. The smaller the caper, the better the quality. Caper berries occur when the plant has been allowed to flower and they taste very similar.

Heat the oil in a large saucepan and fry the onion and garlic until golden.

Add the tomatoes, anchovies, capers and basil and cook, stirring frequently, until the tomatoes are soft, stirring regularly. Season with salt and freshly ground black pepper.

Mix together the ricotta, Parmesan and pecorino and stir into the tomato sauce.

Bring a large saucepan of lightly salted water to the boil and cook the tagliatelle until al dente.

Drain and refresh under cold water, then stir in the tomato sauce.

Preheat the oven to 200°C/400°F/gas mark 6.

Butter a 30 x 20 x 7.5cm (12 x 8 x 2¾in) gratin dish and spoon in the pasta and sauce mixture. Top with slices of mozzarella.

Bake for 10–15 minutes and serve immediately.

Timballo di Maccheroni con i Piccioni

Timballo of Maccheroni with Squabs

Emilia Romagna is known for its very rich food. A lot of dairy products are used, unlike in the southern part of Italy. *Battuto* means 'beaten', so the vegetables must be chopped as finely as possible to give the appearance of having been beaten.

Melt 40g (1½oz) of the butter in a large frying pan and cook the battuto – celery, onion, carrot and pancetta – over a low heat until the vegetables are soft.

Add the squab and fry them until golden all over, then add the wine, a little at a time.

Pour in the stock, season with salt and pepper and add the nutmeg. Simmer over a very low heat until the birds are tender. (There should be a lot of sauce left when the squabs are cooked.) Meanwhile, butter a 26cm (10¼in) round hinged tin.

Make the pasta frolla (page 18). Cut off two-thirds and roll out to a circle large enough to line the tin. Roll out the smaller piece of dough to make a lid and place between two sheets of greaseproof paper or cling film. Chill the pastry-lined tin and the lid in the refrigerator for 30 minutes.

Meanwhile, bring a large saucepan of lightly salted water to the boil and half-cook the penne, then drain.

Make the béchamel sauce using the method on page 16.

Remove the squab from the sauce and set aside to cool. Add the penne to the sauce and finish cooking until al dente. Remove from the heat and set aside to cool.

Remove the meat from the birds and set aside. Discard the bones.

Dice the remaining butter and add it to the pasta with the Parmesan, prosciutto and béchamel sauce. Fold in well.

Preheat the oven to 180°C/350°F/gas mark 4.

Spoon a layer of the pasta mixture into the pastry case and cover with a layer of meat. Scatter over a few shavings of white truffle or a few drops of truffle oil. Continue making layers in this way until all the ingredients have been used. Cover the pasta with the pastry lid and seal well around the edges. Prick the lid with a fork.

Bake for 40–60 minutes. Remove the pie from the oven and leave to rest for 10 minutes, then remove from the tin and serve, cut into wedges.

125g (4½oz) butter, plus extra for greasing

2 squabs (domesticated pigeons), halved

5 tablespoons dry white wine

250ml (9fl oz) meat stock

salt and freshly ground black pepper

pinch of freshly grated nutmeg

375g (12oz) dried penne

4 tablespoons freshly grated Parmesan cheese

100g (3½oz) prosciutto, diced

1 white truffle or truffle oil

FOR THE BÉCHAMEL

50g (2oz) butter

40g (1½oz) flour

500ml (17fl oz) milk, warmed

salt and freshly ground black pepper

pinch of freshly grated nutmeg

FOR THE BATTUTO

1 celery stick, very finely chopped

1 medium onion, very finely chopped

1 carrot, very finely chopped

50g (2oz) pancetta, finely chopped

FOR THE PASTA FROLLA

400g (14oz) plain flour

60g (2½oz) sugar

salt

200g (7oz) butter, diced

4 eggs

juice of ½ lemon

serves 6–8

Timballo di Mezze Zite alla Ceccarius

Timballo of Mezze Zite Ceccaarius

1 quantity Puff Pastry (page 17) OR buy a large ready-made vol-au-vent case

plain flour, for dusting

1 egg, beaten

100ml (3½fl oz) extra virgin olive oil

500g (18oz) plum tomatoes, seeded and diced

salt and freshly ground black pepper

450g (1lb) small octopus or squid, cleaned and thinly sliced

2 garlic cloves, finely chopped

2 tablespoons finely chopped fresh parsley

100g (3½oz) black olives, stoned and sliced

50g (2oz) salted capers, well rinsed

25g (1oz) dried porcini mushrooms, soaked in warm water for 30 minutes, drained and sliced

8 anchovy fillets, preserved in oil

315g (11oz) mezze zite or occhi di lupo

serves 8

This dish was named after Ceccarius who was a specialist in Roman law during the Roman Empire.

Preheat the oven to 230°C/450°F/gas mark 8.

Roll out the puff pastry on a lightly floured surface to about 2cm (¾in) thick. Dip a round or oval vol-au-vent cutter in flour and stamp out the desired shape. Alternatively, cut around a plate using a sharp knife. Cut cleanly without dragging or twisting the pastry. Place on a baking sheet.

Brush the top of the pastry with beaten egg.

Flour a smaller cutter and cut an inner ring, pressing down on the pastry to about half its depth.

Bake for about 15 minutes until the pastry is well-risen and pale brown. Do not open the oven door during cooking, as the cold air may cause the pastry to collapse. When baked, remove the lid and scoop out the soft inside.

Heat 1 tablespoon of olive oil in a frying pan, add the tomatoes and fry, stirring constantly, for 2–3 minutes. Season with salt and pepper, remove from the heat and set aside.

In another frying pan, heat 2 tablespoons of the remaining olive oil and add the octopus or squid. Stew gently for 2 minutes, remove from the heat and set aside.

In a third frying pan, heat the remaining oil, add the garlic, parsley, olives, capers, mushrooms and anchovies and cook until they have completely amalgamated. Remove from the heat and set aside.

Preheat the oven again to 230°C/450°F/gas mark 8.

Meanwhile, bring a large saucepan of lightly salted water to the boil and cook the mezze zite until al dente. Drain and turn into a large bowl. Pour over the tomatoes and add the octopus and the mushroom and olive sauce. Mix well and adjust the seasoning, if necessary.

Spoon the pasta mixture into the vol-au-vent case, place the lid on top and heat in the oven for a few minutes. Serve immediately.

Tortellini in Cassa

Baked Tortellini

salt

350g (12oz) fresh tortellini

20g (¾oz) butter, finely flaked

50g (2oz) freshly grated Parmesan cheese

beaten egg, for brushing

FOR THE PASTA FROLLA

200g (7oz) plain flour, plus extra for dusting

100g (3½oz) butter, plus extra for greasing

1 egg

FOR THE SAUCE

10g (½oz) butter

1 tablespoon extra virgin olive oil

150g (5oz) onion, finely chopped

100g (3½oz) minced pork

50g (2oz) prosciutto crudo, finely chopped

3 tablespoons fresh Passata (page 15), or shop-bought

25g (1oz) dried porcini mushrooms, soaked in lukewarm water for 1 hour, drained and finely chopped

salt and freshly ground black pepper

100ml (3½fl oz) single cream

serves 4–6

Tortellini are a speciality of Bologna and are always served for Christmas dinner. A local legend was made into a play in 1925 by a Bolognese writer, Ostilio Lucarini. It was called *The Man who Invented Tortellini* and tells the story of a cook who saw his employer's naked wife asleep and fell in love with her. As a token of his hopeless passion, he prepared pasta in the shape of her navel to be served at a banquet. One Bolognese journalist, about 130 years ago, wrote: 'Tortellini are more essential than the sun for Sunday, or love for a woman!'

Make the pasta frolla (page 18), then cover with cling film and leave to rest in the refrigerator for 1 hour.

To make the sauce, melt the butter in a frying pan, add the olive oil and gently cook the onion until soft and golden.

Add the minced pork and prosciutto and fry for a few minutes until sealed. Add the passata and the mushrooms. Season with salt and pepper and cook gently for 20 minutes.

Remove from the heat, add the cream and set aside.

Meanwhile, bring a large saucepan of lightly salted water to the boil and cook the tortellini until al dente. Drain and toss in the sauce.

Preheat the oven to 200°C/400°F/gas mark 6. Butter a circular, hinged 20.5cm (8in) tin.

Cut off two-thirds of the pastry, roll out the larger piece on a lightly floured surface and use to line the tin. Spoon the tortellini into the pastry case and add the flaked butter and Parmesan.

Roll out the remaining pastry to make a lid. Cover the filling with the lid and seal the edge well. Brush with the beaten egg.

Bake for 25 minutes. Serve immediately.

Timballo di Taglierini con Carne

Timballo of Taglierini and Meatballs

This is a traditional recipe from Brindisi, Puglia. It is interesting to note that no tomato is used in this recipe, which has a wonderful flavour – a flavour of times forgotten.

First, make the meatballs by combining all the ingredients in a large bowl and mixing well. Dampen your hands and roll small quantities of the mixture into marble-size balls. Set aside. Place the shin of beef, onion, celery, parsley and 4 tablespoons of the olive oil in a heavy-based, flameproof casserole and season with salt and pepper. Add sufficient water to cover the meat and bring to the boil. Reduce the heat and simmer for 1 hour. When the water has reduced by half, add the prosciutto and wine and cook for 1–1½ hours or until the beef is tender, then remove from the heat. Remove the beef from the casserole and reserve for another dish. (It is good sliced, fried quickly in extra virgin olive oil and served with salad.)

Heat the remaining oil in a frying pan and cook the meatballs until golden and cooked through. Add them to the casserole. The sauce should not be too dry.

Bring a large saucepan of lightly salted water to the boil and cook the pasta until al dente. Drain and turn into a large bowl. Stir in 60g (2½oz) of the butter to stop the pasta from sticking. Beat the egg yolks with 4 tablespoons of the Parmesan, add to the pasta and toss well.

Preheat the oven to 180°C/350°F/gas mark 4. Butter a 30cm (12in) gratin dish and sprinkle with 2 tablespoons of the breadcrumbs.

Spoon half the pasta mixture into the dish and top with half the sauce and meatballs. Sprinkle with Parmesan. Add the remaining pasta and the rest of the sauce and cover with the remaining breadcrumbs and Parmesan. Dot the top with the remaining butter. Bake for 20–25 minutes, then serve immediately.

450g (1lb) shin beef, boned and tied with string

1 large onion, finely chopped

1 celery stick, finely chopped

1 small bunch of fresh parsley, finely chopped

6 tablespoons extra virgin olive oil

salt and freshly ground black pepper

40g (1½oz) prosciutto, finely chopped

4 tablespoons white wine

400g (14oz) fresh tagliarini or tagliatelle

100g (3½oz) butter, diced

2 egg yolks

100g (3½oz) freshly grated Parmesan cheese

4 tablespoons fresh breadcrumbs

FOR THE MEATBALLS

200g (7oz) minced beef

2 tablespoons freshly grated Parmesan cheese

1 egg

1 small bunch of fresh parsley, finely chopped

salt and freshly ground black pepper

serves 8

Pasticcio di Spaghetti e Salmone Fumigato Bekendorf

Pasticcio of Spaghetti and Smoked Salmon

75g (3oz) butter, plus extra for greasing

salt

350g (12oz) spaghetti

200g (7oz) smoked salmon, cut in strips

100g (3½oz) freshly grated Parmesan cheese

FOR THE BÉCHAMEL SAUCE

75g (3oz) butter

40g (1½oz) flour

500ml (17fl oz) milk, warmed

pinch of freshly grated nutmeg

salt

serves 4–6

This extremely easy pasta dish was invented by Bekendorf, who was head chef to the last Czar of Russia, Nicholas II, just before the Russian Revolution.

Butter a large gratin dish. Preheat the oven to 180°C/350°F/gas mark 4.

Bring a large saucepan of lightly salted water to the boil and cook the spaghetti until al dente. Drain well, turn into a large bowl and toss with the butter.

Make the béchamel sauce following the method on page 16.

Spoon half the spaghetti into the dish, cover with the smoked salmon, then top with half the béchamel sauce and sprinkle with Parmesan. Add the remaining spaghetti and cover with the remaining béchamel sauce. Sprinkle with the remaining Parmesan and dot with butter.

Bake for 15 minutes. Serve immediately.

Pasticcio di Penne alla Valdostana

Baked Penne with Fontina Cheese and Squash

Val d'Aosta is on the border with France at the foot of Mont Blanc. Fontina is the regional cheese.

Bring a large saucepan of lightly salted water to the boil and cook the penne until al dente. Drain and transfer to a large mixing bowl.

Melt half the butter in a large frying pan over a high heat, then add the onion and garlic and cook, stirring frequently, until the onion is soft.

Add the courgette, squash and pumpkin and season with salt and pepper. Lower the heat and cook, stirring frequently, for about 10 minutes until the pumpkin is tender. Add to the pasta and stir through.

Make the béchamel sauce (page 16).

Preheat the oven to 180°C/350°F/gas mark 4. Butter a deep 2 litre (3½ pint) ovenproof dish.

Add the béchamel sauce and grated fontina to the pasta, and combine well. Spoon the pasta mixture into the dish, sprinkle with the Parmesan and dot with butter.

Bake for about 50 minutes or until the top is brown and bubbly. Leave to rest for a few minutes before serving.

salt

400g (14oz) penne

150g (5oz) butter

1 small onion, finely chopped

1 garlic clove, finely chopped

1 courgette, cut in fine julienne strips

1 medium squash, peeled and cut in fine julienne strips

225g (8oz) pumpkin, peeled, seeded and grated

salt and freshly ground black pepper

225g (8oz) fontina cheese, grated

50g (2oz) freshly grated Parmesan

FOR THE BÉCHAMEL SAUCE

450ml (16fl oz) milk

60g (2½oz) butter

40g (1½oz) flour

salt and freshly ground black pepper

pinch of freshly grated nutmeg

serves 6

Ⓥ

Pasticcio di Pasta Vegetariano

Vegetarian Pasticcio

FOR THE PASTRY

250g (9oz) plain flour, plus extra for dusting

75g (3oz) butter, softened, plus extra for greasing

salt

pinch of freshly grated nutmeg

125ml (4fl oz) milk

2 eggs

FOR THE FILLING

200g (7oz) dried mezze penne

3 tablespoons extra virgin olive oil

2 shallots, finely chopped

1 yellow pepper, seeded and diced

1 red pepper, seeded and diced

12–15 fresh basil leaves, torn

200g (7oz) shelled peas, cooked

salt and freshly ground black pepper

50g (2oz) freshly grated Parmesan cheese

serves 6–8

First, make the pastry. Put the flour in a mound and add the butter, salt and nutmeg. Add the milk, a little at a time, and 1 egg, working the pastry together by hand. Form the pastry into a ball, wrap in cling film and leave to rest in the refrigerator for 30 minutes

To make the filling, bring a large saucepan of lightly salted water to the boil, cook the mezze penne until al dente and drain.

Meanwhile, heat the oil in a frying pan, add the shallots and cook until soft. Add the peppers and basil leaves and cook, stirring occasionally, for about 10 minutes. Add the peas and season with salt and pepper.

Add the pasta and mix together gently with a wooden spoon over a low heat for a few minutes. Remove from the heat and stir in the Parmesan.

Preheat the oven to 200°C/400°F/gas mark 6. Butter a hinged 20.5cm (8in) tin.

Cut off two-thirds of the pastry and roll out on a lightly floured surface, then use to line the tin. Roll out the remaining pastry to make a lid. Pour the pasta mixture into the pastry case, cover it with the lid, seal the edges well and decorate with pastry trimmings. Beat the remaining egg with 1 tablespoon water and brush the lid to glaze.

Bake for 30–40 minutes. Remove the sides from the tin and serve the pasticcio immediately.

Pasticcio di Spaghettini ai Frutti di Mare

Pasticcio of Spaghettini with Seafood

Prepare the seafood. Scrub the clams and mussels under cold water and debeard the mussels. Discard any that do not close when sharply tapped. Put them in a saucepan, cover tightly and cook over a high heat, shaking the pan frequently, for about 5 minutes. As soon as the shells open, remove the saucepan from the heat, discarding any shellfish that have not opened. Remove the clams and mussels from the shells.

Heat the olive oil in a frying pan and toss the shrimps, scallops and prawns for a few minutes until the prawns have changed colour.

To make the sauce, heat the milk in a saucepan to just below boiling point, then remove the pan from the heat.

Melt the butter in another saucepan, then add the flour and stir well. Add the milk, a little at a time, stirring constantly. Season with salt, pepper and nutmeg, stir in the parsley and cook for 15 minutes, whisking occasionally with a balloon whisk to ensure a creamy texture.

Add all the cooked seafood to the sauce.

Preheat the oven to 200°C/400°F/gas mark 6. Butter a large gratin dish and sprinkle with half the breadcrumbs

Bring a large saucepan of lightly salted water to the boil and cook the spaghettini until al dente. Drain, turn into a large bowl, add the seafood mixture and mix well.

Spoon the pasta mixture into the dish, dot the surface with the remaining butter and sprinkle with the remaining breadcrumbs.

Bake for a few minutes or until the top is golden. Serve immediately.

350g (12oz) – COOKED WEIGHT – clams and mussels, shelled; peeled shrimp and prawns, and shelled scallops, halved

2 tablespoons extra virgin olive oil

350g (12oz) spaghettini

40g (1½oz) butter

110–165g (4–6oz) fresh breadcrumbs

FOR THE SAUCE

100ml (3½fl oz) milk

75g (3oz) butter

10g (½oz) flour

salt and freshly ground black pepper

freshly grated nutmeg

3 tablespoons finely chopped fresh parsley

serves 4–6

Pasticcio Duca di Mantova

The Duke of Mantua's Pasticcio

FOR THE PASTA FROLLA

350g (12oz) plain flour, plus extra for dusting

75g (3oz) plus 1 tablespoon sugar

salt

175g (6oz) butter

2 egg yolks

grated rind of ½ lemon

beaten egg, for brushing

FOR THE SAUCE

1 pigeon or partridge

100g (3½oz) sweetbreads

50g (2oz) butter

4 tablespoons olive oil

1 onion, finely chopped

200g (7oz) chicken livers, cleaned and chopped

50g (2oz) dried porcini mushrooms, soaked in boiling water, drained and finely chopped

100g (3½oz) spicy sausage, skinned and chopped

100g (3½oz) prosciutto, finely chopped

200g (7oz) minced pork

2 tablespoons brandy

500ml (18fl oz) fresh Passata (page 15), or shop-bought

175ml (6fl oz) water or stock

salt and freshly ground black pepper

500g (18oz) maccheroncini rigati

75g (3oz) grated Parmesan cheese

serves 8

Mantua is a city that dates back to Etruscan times. It is surrounded by very fertile land. Its most famous son was the poet Virgil (70–19BC), author of *Aeneid*, which he actually wrote in Naples and Sicily. In 1328 the Gonzagas arrived in Mantua after successfully conquering the Bonalcosis. During their supremacy until 1627, many great works of art were created.

Make the pasta frolla (page 18). Wrap in cling film and leave to rest in the refrigerator for 1 hour.

Meanwhile, prepare the sauce. Remove the flesh from the pigeon or partridge and chop it into small pieces.

Place the sweetbreads in a saucepan of boiling water for 10 minutes. Drain and when cool enough to handle, remove and discard the skin and chop into small dice.

Melt the butter with the oil in a frying pan and cook the onion over a low heat until soft and golden.

Add the pigeon or partridge meat, sweetbreads, chicken livers, soaked porcini, sausage, prosciutto and minced pork. Stir frequently until browned.

Add the brandy and cook until evaporated, then add the passata and water or stock. Cover the pan and cook over a low heat for 1 hour. The sauce should be slightly thickened. Season with salt and freshly ground black pepper.

Bring a large saucepan of lightly salted water to the boil and cook the maccheroncini rigati until al dente. Drain, turn into a large bowl, add the sauce and Parmesan and toss well.

Preheat the oven to 200°C/400°F/gas mark 6.

Cut off two-thirds of the pastry, roll out on a lightly floured surface and use to line a 26cm (10¼in) circular springform tin. Roll out the remaining pastry to make a lid.

Spoon the pasta into the pastry case and cover tightly with the pastry lid, then brush the lid with beaten egg.

Bake for 30 minutes. Remove the tin from the oven and leave to rest for 5 minutes before serving.

Timpano di Lasagne al Duca d'Este

Timpano of Lasagne with Fillets of Sole and Shrimp

This dish is traditionally eaten on Good Friday.

Make the pasta (page 10) and roll out into wide sheets. The final setting on the pasta machine should be number 1.

Bring a large pan of lightly salted water to the boil. Cook the pasta sheets, a few at a time, until al dente – about 2 minutes. Drain, drop into cold water, and drain again on clean tea towels.

To make the sauce, pour the water into a pan and add the shrimp or prawn shells, half the wine, the onion, bay leaves and peppercorns. Bring to a gentle boil, reduce the heat and simmer for 10 minutes, crushing the shells occasionally.

Strain the stock, pressing the shells down well to extract as much of the flavour as possible. Discard the shells and set the stock aside.

Melt 100g (3½oz) of the butter in a frying pan, then gently seal the sole fillets on each side. Season with salt and pepper and add the remaining wine. Cook for a few minutes more until the sauce has thickened. Remove from the heat and set aside. Melt the remaining butter in a frying pan and sauté the prawns until they change colour. Pour over the brandy and ignite. Remove from the heat and set aside when the flames have died down.

To make the cheese-béchamel, melt the butter over a low heat, add the flour and mix in thoroughly with a wooden spoon, then gradually add the reserved shellfish stock. Bring the sauce gently to the boil, whisking with a balloon whisk. Cook, whisking constantly, for about 10 minutes until the sauce is silky smooth. Remove from the heat and stir in the Parmesan.

Preheat the oven to 180°C/350°F/gas mark 4.

Butter a 30 x 20 x 7.5cm (12 x 8 x 2¾in) gratin dish and add a layer of pasta, sprinkle on some of the prawns with some of the cooking juices, then a little of the cheese-béchamel. Follow with a layer of pasta, press down with the palm of your hand, then add the sole fillets and some of their cooking juices and top with more cheese-béchamel. Continue making layers in this way, finishing with a layer of pasta topped with the remaining cheese-béchamel. Dot with the butter and bake for 30 minutes or until the top has a beautiful golden crust. Serve.

FOR THE PASTA
350g (12oz) flour

3 eggs

salt

salt

25g (1oz) butter, finely diced, plus extra for greasing

FOR THE SAUCE
500ml (18fl oz) water

500g (18oz) uncooked shrimp or prawns, peeled, shells reserved

250ml (9fl oz) dry white wine

1 small onion, coarsely chopped

2 bay leaves

5 black peppercorns

185g (6½oz) butter

500g (18oz) Dover sole fillets

salt and freshly ground black pepper

2 tablespoons brandy

FOR THE CHEESE-BÉCHAMEL
50g (2oz) butter

50g (2oz) plain flour

100g (3½oz) freshly grated Parmesan cheese

serves 6–8

Pasticcio di Rigatoni all Siciliana

Sicilian Pasticcio of Rigatoni

2 medium aubergines

salt

350g (12oz) rigatoni

250ml (9fl oz) light olive oil

1 small onion, finely chopped

1 garlic clove, finely chopped

6 fresh basil leaves

2 tablespoons extra virgin olive oil

315g (11oz) plum tomatoes, peeled, seeded and diced

150g (5oz) fresh Passata (page 15), or shop-bought

freshly ground black pepper

40g (1½oz) butter

150g (5oz) fontina cheese, thinly sliced

40g (1½oz) freshly grated Parmesan cheese

serves 4–6

In this Sicilian pasticcio it is odd to find fontina cheese which comes from the Val d'Aosta in the north of Italy. I can only presume it is a modern recipe, as in days gone by only local products would have been used.

Thinly slice the aubergines, sprinkle with salt and leave in a colander to drain for 1 hour.

Bring a large saucepan of lightly salted water to the boil and cook the rigatoni until al dente. Drain and rinse under cold, running water.

Pat dry the aubergine slices with kitchen paper. Heat the light olive oil in a large frying pan and fry the aubergine slices until golden. Drain on kitchen paper.

Put the onion, garlic, basil, extra virgin olive oil, tomatoes and passata into a saucepan, and season with salt and pepper. Cook, stirring frequently, for 20 minutes. Remove the onion and garlic.

Preheat the oven to 200°C/400°F/gas mark 6. Butter a deep 25.5 x 20cm (10 x 8in) gratin dish. Spoon a thin layer of sauce on to the base of the dish, then a layer of pasta, followed by a layer of aubergines and a layer of fontina cheese. Continue making layers in this way until all the ingredients are used. Finish with a layer of pasta covered with sauce. Sprinkle with the Parmesan and dot with the remaining butter. Bake for 20 minutes.

Ⓥ

CANNELLONI AND RAVIOLI

03

Cannelloni comes in two forms – dried large tubes or fresh squares of pasta to be boiled and then rolled up. Generally speaking, both are then stuffed with ricotta and spinach or borage, or a meat filling, dressed with béchamel sauce and baked. This pasta originates from Emilia.

Ravioli has been in existance since the end of the fourteenth century. It was developed on board ship as a means of using up the left-overs on long voyages. Whatever was left after a meal was chopped up and stuffed into envelopes of pasta for the next meal. These were called *rabioli* – a Genovese dialect word for 'left-overs' or 'things of little value'. They continued to be called by that name until the beginning of the nineteenth century when they became *ravioli*. In Liguria the shape is square but in Trento, it is cresecent-shaped. Ravioli are also found in a triangular shape.

Cannelloni al Ragú

Cannelloni with Meat Sauce

1¾ quantities Basic Pasta Dough
(page 10)

OR 12–15 x 11.5cm (4½in)
ready-made pasta squares

25g (1oz) butter, diced,
plus extra for greasing

freshly grated Parmesan cheese,
for sprinkling

FOR THE RAGÙ SAUCE

4 tablespoons extra virgin olive oil

1 onion, finely chopped

1 carrot, finely chopped

1 celery stick, finely chopped

315g (11oz) minced beef

200g (7oz) minced pork

salt and freshly ground black pepper

175ml (6fl oz) Marsala

500g (18oz) plum tomatoes, peeled,
seeded and diced

2 tablespoons tomato purée

2 tablespoons finely chopped
fresh parsley

water

50g (2oz) Parma ham, diced

FOR THE BÉCHAMEL SAUCE

500ml (18fl oz) milk

50g (2oz) butter

50g (2oz) plain flour

salt and freshly ground black pepper

freshly grated nutmeg

2 tablespoons freshly grated
Parmesan cheese

serves 6–8

Make the pasta (page 10) and roll out into 11.5cm (4½in) square sheets. The final setting on the pasta machine should be number 1.

To make the ragú sauce, heat the oil in a large pan. Fry the onion, carrot and celery until softened. Add the beef and pork and fry until browned. Season with salt and pepper, add the Marsala and allow to evaporate.

Add the tomatoes, tomato purée, parsley and a little water to moisten, then cook over a low heat for about 1 hour.

Bring a large pan of lightly salted water to the boil. Cook the pasta, a few squares at a time, until al dente – about 2 minutes. Drain, drop into cold water, and drain again on clean tea towels.

Make the béchamel sauce. Heat the milk in a saucepan to just below boiling point, then remove the pan from the heat. Melt the butter in another saucepan, then add the flour and stir well. Add the milk, a little at a time, stirring constantly. Cook the sauce for 15 minutes, whisking occasionally with a balloon whisk to ensure a creamy texture.

Remove the pan from the heat, season with salt, pepper and nutmeg and stir in the Parmesan.

Preheat the oven to 200°C/400°F/gas mark 6.

When the meat sauce is ready, add the Parma ham. Divide the meat filling between the pasta squares, and roll up into tubes. Butter a gratin dish large enough to hold the cannelloni in a single layer and place the cannelloni in it. Pour the béchamel sauce over the cannelloni, dot with butter and sprinkle with Parmesan.

Bake for 20–30 minutes. Serve immediately.

Cannelloni di Pesce

Cannelloni stuffed with fish

This is another traditional fish recipe from the Marche's Adriatic coast.

Make the pasta (page 10) and roll out into 11.5cm (4½in) square sheets. The final setting on the pasta machine should be number 1.

Bring a large pan of lightly salted water to the boil. Cook the pasta, a few squares at a time, until al dente – about 2 minutes. Drain, drop into cold water, and drain again on clean tea towels.

To make the filling, heat the olive oil in a large pan and fry the onion, celery and garlic until softened.

Add all the fish and fry for a further 7 minutes. Remove the pan from the heat, season with salt and pepper and stir in the sage and parsley. Squeeze the milk out of the bread and process the bread with the fish in a food processor until smooth.

To make the sauce, finely dice the aubergines, discarding any soft seedy centres. Sprinkle with salt and leave in a colander for 30 minutes to drain.

Meanwhile, heat half the olive oil in a large pan and fry the onion until softened. Add the tomatoes and cook over a low heat for 30 minutes.

Season with oregano, salt and pepper to taste.

Drain the aubergines and pat dry with kitchen paper. Heat the remaining olive oil in a frying pan until it is smoking, add the aubergines and quickly fry them. Add the tomato sauce and cook for a further 15 minutes. Add the olives.

Preheat the oven to 180°C/350°F/gas mark 4.

Spread the fish mixture over the squares of pasta, then roll up the pasta like a flattened Swiss roll.

Butter a gratin dish large enough to hold the cannelloni in a single layer. Add the cannelloni, cover with the tomato and aubergine sauce, drizzle over the melted butter and sprinkle with the Parmesan.

Bake for 15–20 minutes until a golden crust has formed. Serve immediately.

---

12 x 11.5cm (4½in) fresh or dried pasta squares OR 1¼ quantities Basic Pasta Dough (page 10)

50g (2oz) butter, melted, plus extra for greasing

25g (1oz) freshly grated Parmesan cheese

FOR THE FILLING

50g (2oz) onion, finely chopped

25g (1oz) celery sticks, finely chopped

2 garlic cloves, finely chopped

4 tablespoons extra virgin olive oil

250g (9oz) skinless swordfish fillet, diced

250g (9oz) skinless angler fish fillet, diced

150g (5oz) skinless Dover sole fillet, diced

salt and freshly ground black pepper

1 tablespoon fresh sage, finely chopped

4 tablespoons fresh parsley, finely chopped

4 slices of bread, soaked in milk

FOR THE SAUCE

400g (14oz) aubergines

8 tablespoons extra virgin olive oil

50g (2oz) onion, finely chopped

400g (14oz) ripe plum tomatoes, peeled and coarsely chopped

chopped fresh oregano, to taste

salt and freshly ground black pepper

25g (1oz) black olives, stoned and chopped

serves 6–8

Cannelloni Rossini

Cannelloni with Chicken and Chicken Livers

8 x 11.5cm (4½in) fresh or dried pasta squares OR 1 quantity Basic Pasta Dough (page 10)

butter, for greasing

4 tablespoons fresh Passata (page 15), or shop-bought

FOR THE BÉCHAMEL SAUCE

20g (¾oz) butter

20g (¾oz) flour

450ml (16fl oz) milk, warmed

salt and freshly ground white pepper

FOR THE FILLING

3 tablespoons olive oil

1 medium carrot, finely chopped

1 medium onion, finely chopped

1 celery stick, finely chopped

100g (3½oz) veal, coarsely chopped

100g (3½oz) skinless chicken breast fillet, coarsely chopped

125g (4½oz) chicken livers, coarsely chopped

175ml (6fl oz) Marsala

salt and freshly ground black pepper

20g (¾oz) dried porcini mushrooms, soaked in warm water for 30 minutes and drained, dried and coarsely chopped

2 eggs

pinch of freshly grated nutmeg

50g (2oz) freshly grated Parmesan cheese

serves 4

In 1816, Francesco Barbaia, the famous impresario of the San Carlo Theatre brought Giacchino Rossini to Naples with the promise of letting him live in his house (the Palazzo Berio in Via Toledo), with the use of his cook. In return, Rossini had to deliver a new opera within six months. With some last-minute threats and a ration of only two plates of maccheroni (pasta) a day, Rossini finally produced his famous masterpiece *Othello*.

Make the pasta (page 10) and roll out into 11.5cm (4½in) squares). The final setting on the pasta machine should be number 1.

To make the filling, heat the olive oil in a pan and fry the carrot, onion and celery. Add the veal, chicken breast and livers and fry over a high heat to seal. Pour in the Marsala, season with salt and pepper and add porcini mushrooms. Cook gently until the Marsala has evaporated.

   Transfer the mixture to a food processor and process finely. Scrape into a bowl and stir in the eggs, nutmeg and most of the Parmesan. Preheat the oven to 230°C/450°F/gas mark 8.

Make the béchamel sauce using the method on page 16.

To assemble, divide the meat mixture between the pasta squares and roll up into sausage shapes. Butter a gratin dish large enough to take the cannelloni in a single layer. Arrange the cannelloni in the dish, pour the béchamel sauce over, top with the passata and sprinkle over the reserved Parmesan.

   Bake for 15 minutes and serve immediately.

Cannelloni Etrusco

Etruscan Cannelloni

The Etruscans settled in Tuscany in the tenth century BC, reaching their peak between the eighth and the fifth centuries BC. They represent the first Italic civilisation with the necessary energy to undertake a policy of expansion.

Make the pasta (page 10) and roll out into 10cm (4in) squares. The final setting on the pasta machine should be number 1.

Bring a large pan of lightly salted water to the boil. Cook the pasta squares, a few at a time, until al dente – about 2 minutes. Drain, drop into cold water, and drain again on clean tea towels.

Make the béchamel sauce using the method on page 16.

To make the filling, heat the olive oil in a large pan and fry the mushrooms. Reserve two-thirds of the béchamel sauce and stir the mushrooms into the remainder. Add Parma ham and Parmesan, season with salt and pepper and fold in well.

Preheat oven to 230°C/450°F/gas Mark 8.

Place a generous spoonful of this mixture on each square of pasta and roll up. Butter a gratin dish large enough to hold the cannelloni in a single layer. Place the cannelloni in the dish.

Add the milk to the reserved béchamel sauce and reheat. Pour the sauce over the cannelloni and sprinkle with the Parmesan and Gruyère.

Bake for 15 minutes. Serve immediately.

FOR THE PASTA

200g (7oz) Farina – flour or strong plain white flour

1 egg

1 egg yolk

salt

butter, for greasing

250ml (9fl oz) milk

50g (2oz) freshly grated Gruyère cheese

50g (2oz) freshly grated Parmesan cheese

FOR THE BÉCHAMEL SAUCE

50g (2oz) butter

50g (2oz) flour

500ml (17fl oz) milk, warmed

salt

FOR THE FILLING

2 tablespoons extra virgin olive oil

315g (11oz) wild mushrooms, sliced (preferably mixed, but porcini will do)

50g (2oz) Parma ham cut in julienne strips

3 tablespoons freshly grated Parmesan cheese

salt and freshly ground black pepper

serves 4

Cannelloni di Ricotta e Prosciutto Crudo

Cannelloni with Ricotta and Prosciutto

FOR THE PASTA

315g (11oz) flour

3 eggs

salt

OR 12 x 11.5cm (4½in) fresh pasta squares

40g (1½oz) butter, melted, plus extra for greasing

450ml (16fl oz) fresh Passata (page 15), or shop-bought

60g (2¼oz) freshly grated Parmesan cheese, plus extra to serve

FOR THE FILLING

700g (1½lb) ricotta

3 eggs

2 egg yolks

2 tablespoons chopped fresh parsley

200g (7oz) freshly grated Parmesan cheese

salt and freshly ground black pepper

freshly grated nutmeg

18 slices prosciutto crudo

serves 8–10

Ricotta, which means 're-cooked', is made from the whey left over from making pecorino cheese. It is a rich, fresh cheese – slightly grainy, but smoother than cottage cheese. Real ricotta is made from sheep's milk, but cow's milk ricotta is more readily available. Try and get sheep's milk ricotta – it is quite different. When Ann first went to the Marche in 1963, shepherds used to bring their ricotta cheeses in lovely little wicker baskets to sell in the markets; if you got there early, they would still be warm.

Make the pasta (page 10) and roll out into 18 x 9cm (3½in) squares. The final setting on the pasta machine should be number 1.

Bring a large pan of lightly salted water to the boil. Cook the pasta squares, a few at a time, until al dente – about 2 minutes. Drain, drop into cold water, and drain again on clean tea towels.

To make the filling, mix together the ricotta, eggs, egg yolks, parsley and 100g (3½oz) Parmesan. Season with salt, pepper and nutmeg to taste.

Preheat the oven to 180°C/350°F/gas mark 4.

Put a slice of prosciutto on each pasta square. Divide the cheese mixture between the pasta squares and roll up into tubes.

Butter a gratin dish large enough to hold the cannelloni in a single layer. Arrange the cannelloni the dish. Drizzle over the melted butter, cover with the passata and sprinkle with the remaining Parmesan.

Bake for 20–30 minutes. Serve immediately, with extra Parmesan.

Cannelloni al Forno Modenese

Modenese Cannelloni

12 x 11.5cm (4½ in) fresh
pasta squares – 1¾ quantities
Basic Pasta Dough (page 10)

25g (1oz), butter diced, plus extra
for greasing

FOR THE BÉCHAMEL SAUCE
100g (3½ oz) butter
40g (1½oz) flour
500ml (18fl oz) milk, warmed
pinch of freshly grated nutmeg

FOR THE FILLING
2 tablespoons extra virgin olive oil
100g (3½ oz) minced lean beef
100g (3½ oz) minced veal
100g (3½ oz) minced chicken
100g (3½ oz) Parma ham, finely
chopped
50g (2oz) freshly grated Parmesan
cheese

serves 6

The French author Stendhal wrote in 1816, 'I lunched at Modena, the cleanest and gayest Italian city that I have visited so far!'

Make the pasta (page 10) and roll out into 11.5cm (4½in) squares. The final setting on the pasta machine should be number 1.

Bring a large pan of lightly salted water to the boil. Cook the pasta squares, a few at a time, until al dente – about 2 minutes. Drain, drop into cold water, and drain again on clean tea towels.

To make the filling, heat the oil in a pan and cook the minced meats for about 10 minutes, adding a little water as necessary. When cooked, add the Parma ham and Parmesan.

Make the béchamel sauce using the method on page 16. Reserve a little less than half the sauce and add the remainder to the meat mixture and mix together.

Preheat the oven to 180°C/350°F/gas mark 4.

Divide the filling between the pasta squares and roll up into tubes. Butter a gratin dish large enough to hold the cannelloni in a single layer. Arrange the cannelloni in the dish. If the reserved béchamel sauce has become a little too thick to pour, beat in a little more milk before pouring it over the pasta. Dot the surface with butter and bake until the top is lightly golden. Serve immediately.

Cannelloni alla Pesarese

Cannelloni Pesaro–style

Pesaro is an attractive seaside town with a thriving fishing port. It was here that composer and pasta-lover Rossini was born and every year a Rossini festival is held in August.

Make the pasta (page 10) and roll out into 11.5cm (4½in) squares. The final setting on the pasta machine should be number 1.

Bring a large pan of lightly salted water to the boil. Cook the pasta squares, a few at a time, until al dente – about 2 minutes. Drain, drop into cold water, and drain again on clean tea towels.

To make the filling, melt the butter with the olive oil in a pan. Add the meats and cook, stirring occasionally, until sealed, then season with salt and pepper. Add the water and cook until tender.

Meanwhile, make the béchamel sauce following the method on page 16, and reserve.

When the meat is cooked, mince it and return to the pan, set over a low heat. Add the Parmesan, egg, tomato purée, nutmeg, and cream and cook for 10 minutes. Remove from the heat and add the fontina and Gruyère. Mix in well.

Preheat the oven to 200°C/400°F/gas mark 6.

Divide the filling between the squares and roll up to form tubes. Butter a gratin dish large enough to hold the cannelloni in a single layer. Arrange the cannelloni in the dish. Dot with the butter and pour over the béchamel sauce.Sprinkle with the grated Parmesan.

Bake for 40 minutes. Serve immediately.

12 x 11.5cm (4½in) fresh pasta squares – 1¾ quantities Basic Pasta Dough (page 10)

50g (2oz) butter, diced, plus extra for greasing

50g (2oz) freshly grated Parmesan cheese

FOR THE BÉCHAMEL SAUCE

25g (1oz) butter

25g (1oz) flour

500ml (17fl oz) milk, warmed

salt

pinch of nutmeg

FOR THE FILLING

25g (1oz) butter

2 tablespoons extra virgin olive oil

150g (5oz) pork loin, coarsely chopped

150g (5oz) rump steak, coarsely chopped

salt and freshly ground black pepper

250ml (9fl oz) water

50g (2oz) freshly grated Parmesan cheese

1 egg

2 tablespoons tomato purée

pinch of freshly grated nutmeg

250ml (9fl oz) plus 2 tablespoons single cream

75g (3oz) fontina cheese, finely diced

75g (3oz) Gruyère cheese, finely diced

serves 6–8

Cannelloni in Bianco

Cannelloni with ricotta and mozzarella

Make the pasta (page 10) and roll out into 11.5cm (4½in) squares. The final setting on the pasta machine should be number 1.

To make the sauce, heat the olive oil in a large pan and fry the carrots and garlic for a few minutes. Add the tomatoes, season with salt and cook over a moderate heat for 15 minutes. Add the milk and cook until the sauce has thickened. Remove from the heat.

Bring a large pan of lightly salted water to the boil. Cook the pasta squares, a few at a time, until al dente – about 2 minutes. Drain, drop into cold water, and drain again on clean tea towels.

To make the filling, beat the egg yolks and egg white with a little salt and add to the ricotta with the Parmesan, mozzarella and salami. Season with freshly ground black pepper and check the salt.

Preheat the oven to 180°C/350°F/gas mark 4.

Divide the filling between the pasta squares and roll up. Butter a gratin dish large enough to hold the cannelloni in a single layer. Spoon some of the sauce on the base of the dish and place the cannelloni on top. Cover with the remaining sauce, sprinkle with grated Parmesan and dot with butter.

Bake for 10–15 minutes. Serve immediately.

12 x 11.5cm (4½in) fresh pasta squares – 1¾ quantities Basic Pasta Dough (page 10)

25g (1oz) butter, diced, plus extra for greasing

20g (¾oz) freshly grated Parmesan cheese

FOR THE SAUCE

4 tablespoons extra virgin olive oil

150g (5oz) carrots, finely chopped

1 garlic clove, finely chopped

400g (14oz) tomatoes, peeled, seeded and finely diced

salt

100ml (3½fl oz) milk, warmed

FOR THE FILLING

2 egg yolks

1 egg white

salt and freshly ground black pepper

185g (6½oz) ricotta cheese

25g (1oz) freshly grated Parmesan

225g (8oz) mozzarella cheese, thinly sliced

40g (1½oz) salami, cut in thin strips

serves 4

Panzarotti

Deep-fried stuffed pasta triangles

1 egg, beaten with 1 teaspoon water

oil, for deep-frying

grated Parmesan cheese, for sprinkling

FOR THE PASTA

600g (1¼lb) plain flour, plus extra for dusting

salt

150ml (¼ pint) olive oil

4 egg yolks

2–3 tablespoons warm water

FOR THE FILLING

175g (6oz) fresh ricotta cheese

175g (6oz) mozzarella cheese, finely diced

6 tablespoons freshly grated Parmesan cheese

60g (2½oz) Parma ham or salami, minced

salt and freshly ground black pepper

freshly grated nutmeg

serves 6

These morsels are served as an appetiser with pre-dinner drinks. If you are short of time, wonton wrappers (obtainable from oriental supermarkets) can be used in place of the pasta dough. These also give a lighter and crisper result. Simply seal with beaten egg and press the edges together. Deep-fry in the same way.

To make the pasta. Sift the flour on to a pastry board and make a well in the centre. Add 2 pinches of salt, the oil and egg yolks and 2 tablespoons of the warm water. Knead the mixture into a firm dough, adding a little more water if necessary. Knead the dough thoroughly until smooth and elastic, then put in a polythene bag and leave it to rest in the refrigerator for about 30 minutes.

To make the filling, mix the ricotta, mozzarella and Parmesan with the Parma ham or salami. Season to taste with salt, pepper and a pinch of freshly grated nutmeg.

To assemble the panzarotti, roll out the dough on a floured board to 2mm (⅟₁₆in) thick, and cut into 7.5cm (2¾in) squares. Place a heaped teaspoon of filling in the centre of each square of pasta. Brush the edges of the pasta with the beaten egg and fold corner-to-corner to make a triangle. Seal the edges lightly together using a fork. Heat the oil for deep-frying to 180–190°C/350–375°F/gas mark 4–5 or until a cube of day-old bread browns in 30 seconds.

Deep-fry the triangles until puffed up, lightly golden and crisp. Drain well on absorbent kitchen paper and serve hot, sprinkled with Parmesan cheese.

Ravioli di Baccala

Ravioli Stuffed with Salt Cod

In the Decameron (1349–51), Boccaccio writes, '…the district is called Bengodi, and there they bind the vines with sausages. And a denier will buy a goose and a gosling into the bargain, and on a mountain, all of grated Parmesan cheese, dwell folk that do nought else but make macaroni and ravioli, and boil them in capon's broth, and then throw them down to be scrambled for'.

First, desalt the cod for the filling. Wash it well under cold running water, then place in a colander, skin side up, and soak in a large bowl of cold water for 3 days, changing the water regularly times. The fish must be submerged all the time.

Make the pasta (page 10) and roll out into 4 portions. The final setting on the pasta machine should be number 1. Keep the dough covered with a damp cloth until required.

To make the filling, drain the salt cod and pat dry. Remove all the bones and cut the flesh into cubes. Bring a saucepan of water to the boil and cook the cod until soft. Drain thoroughly. Place the cod with the garlic in a food processor and process until smooth. With the motor running, gradually add the olive oil through the feeder tube to make a smooth purée.

To make the sauce, heat the olive oil in a frying pan, add the garlic and tomatoes and stir. Add the marjoram, season with salt and pepper and cook gently, stirring frequently, for 10 minutes.

To assemble the ravioli, brush a sheet of pasta with the beaten egg. Place teaspoons of the salt cod purée on the sheet, spaced evenly apart. Place another sheet of pasta on top and press down firmly around the filling. Cut into ravioli with a fluted round pastry cutter or a pastry wheel. Continue in this way until all the ingredients are used.

Bring a large saucepan of lightly salted water to the boil. Cook the ravioli until just under al dente. Drain, using a slotted spoon, and add to the sauce. Cook in the sauce for a further 2 minutes and serve.

1 egg, beaten with 1 teaspoon water

FOR THE PASTA
400g (14oz) Farina O or strong plain white flour
salt
4 eggs

FOR THE FILLING
500g (18oz) dried salt cod
4 garlic cloves
175ml (6fl oz) extra virgin olive oil

FOR THE SAUCE
4 tablespoons extra virgin olive oil
1 garlic clove, finely chopped
6 plum tomatoes, peeled, seeded and diced
leaves from 1 fresh marjoram sprig
salt and freshly ground black pepper

serves 6–8

Ravioli di Zucca con Salsa di Noce

Pasta Envelopes with Pumpkin Filling & Walnut Sauce

These succulent, pumpkin-filled ravioli are delicious with a walnut sauce, but can also be served with melted butter infused with fresh sage.

Make the pasta (page 10) and roll out. The final setting on the pasta machine should be number 1. Cut it into 10cm (4in) squares. Preheat the oven to 180°C/350°F/gas mark 4.

To make the filling, cut the pumpkin in half and remove the seeds and stringy fibres. Place the halves, cut side down, on a baking tray and bake for about 45 minutes or until soft. Alternatively, cook in the microwave for about 10 minutes.

Remove the pumpkin from the oven and let it cool sufficiently to handle. Peel off the skin and leave the flesh to drain in a sieve for 1 hour.

Process the pumpkin to a purée in a food processor or mash with a fork. Leave to drain in a sieve to remove excess water.

Transfer the pumpkin purée to a bowl and add the Parmesan and nutmeg and season with salt and pepper. Blend to a smooth consistency.

To make the walnut sauce, finely chop the walnuts by hand. (A food processor is not suitable for this – it crushes the walnuts too much.) Add the rest of the sauce ingredients and mix together.

To assemble the ravioli, put a heaped teaspoon of the pumpkin mixture on one half of each the square and fold over diagonally. Brush a little beaten egg round the edges of the pasta triangles to seal. (This is a moist filling, so the envelopes cannot be kept too long before cooking.)

Bring a large pan of lightly salted water to the boil and cook the ravioli for about 1 minute. When they rise to the top of the pan, check that they are al dente, then drain.

Serve the ravioli with walnut sauce and grated Parmesan.

FOR THE PASTA

450g (1lb) Farina O flour

5 large eggs

pinch of salt

egg wash for sealing

FOR THE FILLING

Pumpkin, weighing about 900g (2lb) before cleaning

175g (6oz) freshly grated Parmesan cheese

teaspoon freshly grated nutmeg

salt and freshly ground white pepper

WALNUT SAUCE

24–30 walnut halves

2 cloves garlic, crushed

1 generous bunch parsley, finely chopped

1 pinch dried chilli flakes

175ml (6fl oz) extra virgin olive oil

salt and freshly ground black pepper

serves 4–6

Ⓥ

SPAGHETTI

04

It is hard to believe that the word spaghetti, as the description of a type of pasta, has been officially in existence only since 1824. Apparently, it appeared written for the first time in a poem called *Li maccheroni a Napoli* by Antonio Viviani. However, it had probably been used colloquially by the local people before then. The word *spaghetto*, for one strand, is the diminutive of *spago*, meaning string. Spaghetti is made from durum wheat flour and water. Although it was one of the last types of pasta to appear at that time, it quickly became famous. To the rest of the world, spaghetti represents Naples, if not the whole of Italy.

Spaghettini alla Posillipo

Spaghetti with Seafood

750g (1lb 10oz) fresh mussels

750g (1lb 10oz) fresh cockles

350g (12oz) raw Dublin bay prawn tails or prawns

2 small squid, cleaned

3 tablespoons extra virgin olive oil

1 small onion, peeled and finely chopped

2 garlic cloves, finely chopped

175ml (6fl oz) dry white wine

200g (7oz) cherry tomatoes, halved

2 tablespoons finely chopped fresh parsley, plus extra to garnish

pinch of chilli powder

salt and freshly ground black pepper

350g (12oz) spaghettini

serves 4

We ate this dish at a restaurant in Naples at the top of La Forcella in the Camorra district. The Camorra are the Neapolitan equivalent of the Sicilian Mafia, and while the food was very good indeed, the dish was perhaps made more memorable by the setting: when we left the restaurant around midnight, small children were still selling contraband cigarettes and older people were dealing drugs…

Scrub the mussels and cockles under cold running water and discard any that do not close when sharply tapped. Cook in a saucepan, without any extra liquid, over medium heat until the shells open.

Remove the shellfish from the pan with a slotted spoon and discard any that remain shut. Reserve a few mussels and cockles for garnish and remove the remainder from their shells. Strain and reserve the cooking liquid.

Bring a saucepan of salted water to the boil and add the prawns. When the water returns to the boil, strain the prawns and plunge into cold water. This prevents the prawns from overcooking. Remove and discard the shells.

Slice the squid into thin rings.

Heat the olive oil in a frying pan and fry the onion and garlic until golden. Add the squid and cook gently for a few minutes. Add the reserved cooking liquid and wine and reduce over a brisk heat until it forms a glaze. Add the shellfish, prawns, tomato halves, parsley, chilli powder and pepper to taste. Add salt to taste if necessary.

Bring a large saucepan of lightly salted water to the boil and cook the spaghettini until al dente. Drain and place in a large, warmed serving dish. Mix in the seafood sauce and sprinkle with finely chopped parsley. Serve immediately.

Vermicelli alle Vongole in Bianco

Vermicelli with Clams

Fish, an ancient symbol of Christianity, was associated particularly with Fridays because that was the day Christ was crucified. Later on, it became associated with any day of fasting or penance. This recipe comes from Naples and is traditionally eaten on Christmas Eve – a day of fasting.

Wash the clams thoroughly in a bowl under cold running water to get rid of the sand inside the shells. As soon as no sand is left in the bowl, you know that they are clean. Discard any that do not close when sharply tapped.

Heat the olive oil in a large frying pan and briefly fry the garlic. Add the clams and cover with a lid. As soon as the shells open, remove from the heat.

Remove the clams from the pan with a slotted spoon, discarding any that have not opened. Reserve about half the clams and remove the remainder from their shells. Strain the cooking liquid through a very fine sieve. Return all the clams and the cooking liquid to the frying pan together with the chilli flakes.

Meanwhile, bring a large saucepan of lightly salted water to the boil and cook the vermicelli until very al dente. Drain and add to the cooked clams over a very brisk heat. Stir for 2 minutes so that pasta absorbs the broth and flavour of the clams and finishes cooking. Turn into a large, warmed serving dish and serve immediately.

1.2kg (3lb) vongole or other very small clams
150ml (¼ pint) extra virgin oil
2 garlic cloves, finely chopped
a pinch of chilli flakes
500g (18oz) vermicelli

serves 4

Maccheroncini con Brodetto di Gamberi

Prawns in Saffron and Garlic Sauce with Maccheroncini

900g (2lb) unpeeled raw tiger prawns or Mediterranean prawns

125ml (4fl oz) extra virgin olive oil

4 garlic cloves, finely chopped

4 level tablespoons tomato purée

salt and freshly ground black pepper

450ml (16fl oz) dry white wine

a pinch of saffron threads, soaked in 450ml (16fl oz) warm water

400g (14oz) Campofilone maccheroncini or vermicelli

1 tablespoon chopped fresh flat leaf parsley

serves 4

Campofilone is a small medieval town situated on a hill, which faces the Adriatic Sea. This very fine pasta is made by hand there, using 10 eggs for every kilogram of flour. It is said that the pasta is as fine as a cherub's golden hair. From 6–8 August, the people of Campofilone hold a *sagra* (festival) for the pasta with stalls selling dishes of maccheroncini cooked in as many ways as possible. Campofilone maccheroncini is available from Italian delicatessens.

Prepare the prawns by cutting them open down the curved back, without cutting right through, and opening them like a book. Remove and discard the dark intestinal vein.

Heat the olive oil in a frying pan, add the garlic and fry until lightly coloured. Add the prawns and tomato purée and fry briskly until the prawns have turned pink. Season generously with salt and pepper.

Add the wine and boil until it has evaporated. Add the saffron and water mixture and stir, then cook for a few more minutes. Remove the prawns and keep warm. Cook the sauce until it is reduced and thickened.

Meanwhile, bring a large saucepan of lightly salted water to the boil. Cook the maccheroncini or vermicelli briefly until al dente, then drain. Pour the sauce over the prawns, toss the maccheroncini pasta into the prawn sauce, and place in a large, warmed serving dish. Sprinkle with parsley and serve immediately.

Spaghetti alle Alghe con Salmone

Spaghetti with Salmon and Samphire

Samphire is a wild vegetable that grows on salt marshes. It is wonderfully salty and succulent and has a taste of the sea. It is also good eaten raw, dressed with oil and lemon juice. It can be bought from some fishmongers.

Wash the samphire thoroughly under cold running water. Meanwhile bring a saucepan of water to the boil. Drop in the samphire and blanch for 1 minute. Drain in a colander and set aside.

Bring a large saucepan of lightly salted water to the boil, cook the spaghetti until al dente, drain and turn into a large, warmed serving dish.

Meanwhile, melt the butter with the olive oil in a frying pan and cook the shallots and garlic until light golden. Add the white wine and boil until reduced by half. Season with the lemon juice, salt, if needed, and pepper.

Add the salmon to the sauce and stir to mix, then immediately pour the sauce over the spaghetti and toss well together. Add the fresh tomato cubes and samphire and toss well, then serve immediately.

200g (7oz) fresh samphire

250–350g (9–12oz) spaghetti

25g (1oz) butter

4 tablespoons olive oil

2 shallots, finely chopped

1 garlic clove, finely chopped

100ml (3½fl oz) dry white wine

juice of ½ lemon

salt and freshly ground
black pepper

2 salmon fillets, 400g (14oz) total
weight, cut into 1cm (½in) cubes

200g (7oz) plum tomatoes, peeled,
seeded and diced

serves 4–6

Spaghetti con le Polpette

Spaghetti with Meatballs

plain flour, for dusting

400g (14oz) minced lean beef

1 medium onion, finely chopped

1 medium potato, boiled, drained and passed through a potato ricer or food mill while still hot

1 egg

1 small bunch of fresh parsley, finely chopped

salt and freshly ground black pepper

5 tablespoons extra virgin olive oil

400g (14oz) fresh Passata (page 15), or shop-bought

2 tablespoons tomato purée

10 fresh basil leaves

400g (14oz) spaghetti

freshly grated Parmesan cheese, to garnish

serves 6

Cesare Marchi wrote in his book *Quando siamo a Tavola* (When We Are at Table): 'There is an ancient rite all over the meridien, which is repeated simultaneously day after day. As though from an invisible director, millions of husbands, without each other knowing it, telephone to their wives saying, "I'm arriving soon, put the pasta on".' The singer Mario Lanza said that it was spaghetti that made him sing, while Mario Puzo, author of *The Godfather*, claimed that 'Seven days without a plate of spaghetti drops me into a deep, dark well of physical anxiety.'

Spread out the flour on a plate. Mix the beef, onion, potato, egg and parsley in a bowl and season with salt and pepper to taste. When the ingredients are thoroughly combined, dampen your hands and shape into balls the size of large marbles then roll in the flour.

Heat the oil in a frying pan and fry the meatballs until golden all over. Add the passata, tomato purée and two of the basil leaves and cook until the sauce is reduced.

Meanwhile, bring a large saucepan of lightly salted water to the boil. Cook the spaghetti until al dente, then drain. Add the spaghetti to the meatball sauce and toss for a minute or so to coat.

Turn into a large, warmed serving dish. Shred the remaining basil leaves, sprinkle them over the spaghetti with freshly grated Parmesan cheese and serve immediately.

Ⓥ

Spaghetti con Crema di Tartufo e Fiori di Zucchini

Spaghetti with Truffle Paste and Courgette Flowers

This recipe came from a restaurant near Imola, a town famous for Formula One racing. It was late and we were desperately hungry, so we apologetically asked at a wayside restaurant if they could provide a meal. They were willing, providing we did not mind eating something knocked up by the proprietor, as the chef had gone home. He 'knocked up' this pasta for us. White truffle paste is available from Italian delicatessens.

350g (12oz) spaghetti

8 courgette flowers with tiny courgettes attached, no bigger than 5cm (2in) long

100g (3½oz) butter

1 garlic clove, finely chopped

4 tablespoons white truffle paste

salt and freshly ground white pepper

freshly grated Parmesan cheese

1 white truffle (optional)

serves 4

Wash the courgette flowers, remove and discard the stamens and cut the vegetable part into thin slices, leaving a tiny piece attached to the flower. Cut the flower into single petals.

Melt the butter over a low heat and add the garlic and courgette flowers and slices. Cook gently for a few minutes. Be careful not to overcook them, they must still have a bite to them.

Meanwhile, bring a large saucepan of lightly salted water to the boil, cook the spaghetti until al dente, and drain.

Stir in the truffle paste and add the spaghetti. Toss well in the sauce and season with salt and pepper. Turn into a large, warmed serving dish and sprinkle with Parmesan. If you have a white truffle, shave it over the top – the result is magical. Serve immediately.

Spaghetti con Aglio, Olio e Diavolicchio

Spaghetti with Garlic, Oil and Chilli

salt

350g (12oz) spaghetti

3 tablespoons extra virgin olive oil

2 garlic cloves, finely chopped

1 hot red chilli, seeded and finely chopped or good pinch of dried chilli flakes

1 tablespoon finely chopped fresh parsley

serves 4

The ghetto of Naples is where this recipe originated. In Southern Italy the chilli is known as *diavolicchio* (little devil), *peperoncino* being its formal name.

Bring a large saucepan of lightly salted water to the boil, cook the spaghetti until al dente and drain.

Meanwhile, gently heat the olive oil in a frying pan. Add the garlic and chilli, toss in the drained spaghetti and remove from the heat.

Toss in the parsley and turn into a large, warmed serving dish. Serve immediately.

Ⓥ Ⓥ

Bigoli in Salsa all'Ebraica con Acciuge

Bigoli with Anchovies

This is another Venetian ghetto recipe. Franco's mother often made this dish, but also added cooked purple sprouting broccoli and chilli flakes. Instead of a lot of pepper, she used just a touch.

Bring a large saucepan of lightly salted water to the boil, cook the bigoli until al dente, drain and turn into a large bowl.

As the pasta is cooking, heat 3 tablespoons of extra virgin olive oil in a non-stick frying pan. Add the garlic, stir, then add the anchovy fillets. Stir with a wooden spoon until the anchovies have almost disintegrated.

Add the sauce to the pasta with the rest of the oil, the parsley and plenty of freshly ground black pepper. Serve hot or cold.

salt and freshly ground black pepper

450g (1lb) bigoli (page 108) or wholemeal spaghetti

6 tablespoons extra virgin olive oil

5 garlic cloves, finely chopped

18 anchovy fillets in olive oil, drained and coarsely chopped

1 large bunch of fresh flat leaf parsley, finely chopped

serves 6

Spaghetti all'Astice

Spaghetti with Lobster Sauce

1 live lobster, weighing about
800g (1¾lb)

125ml (4fl oz) extra virgin olive oil

2 sun-dried tomatoes in oil,
drained and finely chopped

1 garlic clove, finely chopped

2 tablespoons finely chopped
fresh flat leaf parsley, plus extra
to garnish (optional)

1 fresh chilli, seeded and
thinly chopped

5 tablespoons dry white wine

4 ripe tomatoes, peeled, seeded
and diced

salt

350g (12oz) spaghetti

serves 4

This pasta recipe is an Italian way of making an expensive ingredient, in this case lobster, go further.

Bring a large saucepan of water to the boil and plunge the lobster into it. Return to the boil and cook the lobster for 5 minutes. Remove the lobster from the pot and plunge it into cold water to cool it quickly. Twist off the claws, crack them and remove the meat. Cut open the tail shell, cutting down the length of the soft underside. Remove the meat from the shell, discarding the stomach sac and dark central vein, and cut the into cubes.

Heat the olive oil in a frying pan and fry the sun-dried tomatoes, garlic, parsley and chilli. Add the wine and allow to evaporate. Add the diced tomatoes and cook for 20 minutes, stirring frequently. Season with salt, then remove the sauce from the heat and keep hot.

Meanwhile, bring a large saucepan of lightly salted water to the boil. Cook the spaghetti until al dente. Drain and place in a large warm serving dish.

Add the lobster meat to the sauce, then pour over the spaghetti and mix in well. Sprinkle with more chopped parsley, if liked and serve immediately.

Spaghetti con Pomodori Secchi

Spaghetti with Sun-dried tomatoes, Garlic and Chilli

Garlic was important to the Romans and was considered a strengthening food for soldiers. The Roman poet, Horace, wrote of 'garlic more harmful than hemlock' that could drive one's lover to refuse a kiss and to retreat to the far side of the bed. However, Apicius, the author of a cookery book *De Re Coquinaria Libri Decem*, written in the first half of the first century AD, makes only two mentions of garlic in his recipes and one of them is for invalids.

Bring a large saucepan of lightly salted water to the boil and cook the spaghetti until al dente. Meanwhile, mix all the sauce ingredients together in a frying pan. When the spaghetti is almost ready, heat the sauce until hot, but not boiling.

Drain the spaghetti and toss it well in the sauce. Turn into a large, warmed serving dish and serve immediately.

350g (12oz) spaghetti

FOR THE SAUCE

12–14 sun-dried tomatoes in olive oil, drained and cut into julienne strips

3 garlic cloves, finely chopped

good pinch of dried chilli flakes

salt and freshly ground black pepper

5 tablespoons extra virgin olive oil

1 tablespoon finely chopped flat leaf parsley

serves 4

Ⓥ Ⓥ

Spaghetti nei Peperoni alla Napolitana

Neapolitan Stuffed Peppers

12 large yellow peppers

150ml (¼ pint) extra virgin olive oil

1 garlic clove, finely chopped

150g (5oz) black olives, stoned and sliced

75g (3oz) salted capers, rinsed and chopped

75g (3oz) sultanas

75g (3oz) pine nuts

salt

500g (18oz) spaghetti

25g (1oz) fresh breadcrumbs

serves 12

Neapolitans say a day without pasta is a day without food.

Peel the peppers by holding them over a flame or grilling them until the skins have turned black and bubbled. Peel off the skins, taking care not to break the peppers.

Heat 2 tablespoons of the oil in a frying pan and briefly fry the garlic, olive slices and capers. Remove the frying pan from the heat and add the sultanas and pine nuts.

Bring a large saucepan of lightly salted water to the boil. Cook the spaghetti until just under al dente and drain.

Toss the spaghetti into the sauce.

Preheat the oven to 180°C/350°F/gas mark 4.

Cut the stalk end off the peppers to make a lid. Remove the seeds and white membranes from inside.

Fill each pepper with 3 forkfuls of spaghetti and sauce. Place the pepper lids on top.

Drizzle a little extra virgin olive oil on the base of a gratin dish large enough to hold the peppers in a single layer. Place the peppers in the dish, drizzle over the remaining olive oil and any oil left from the spaghetti sauce. Bake for 40 minutes.

Remove the dish from the oven, sprinkle with the breadcrumbs and return to the oven for a further 10 minutes. Serve immediately.

Ⓥ Ⓥ

Spaghetti con Rosmarino

Spaghetti with Rosemary

salt

350g (12oz) spaghetti

3 tablespoons extra virgin olive oil

3 garlic cloves, finely chopped

½ handful tiny rosemary sprigs

freshly grated Parmesan cheese,
to serve (optional)

serves 4

Rosemary belongs to the mint family and is native to the Mediterranean. According to folklore, the Virgin Mary draped her cloak over a rosemary bush and placed a white flower on top of it. In the morning, the flower had turned blue so after that, the plant was called Rose of Mary.

Bring a large saucepan of lightly salted water to the boil and cook the spaghetti until al dente and drain.

Meanwhile, gently heat the olive oil in a frying pan. Add the garlic and rosemary, toss in the spaghetti and remove from the heat.

Season with salt and turn into a large, warmed serving dish. Serve immediately. If you like, Parmesan cheese can be served with this dish.

Ⓥ

Spaghetti in Bianco con Tartufi alla Rossini

Spaghetti with Truffles

freshly ground black pepper

400g (14oz) spaghetti

large knob of butter

1 white truffle

freshly grated Parmesan cheese

serves 4

Tartufi – truffles – of one species or another are available all year round in the Marche. From the beginning of October to the middle of December is the season for the famed *tartufo bianco pregiato*, the white truffle so highly prized by the Italians. It has a strong, distinctive aroma that is difficult to describe. This may seem an extravagant dish, but if you can get hold of a white truffle, it is well worth it. The more generous you are with the truffle the better the dish.

Ths dish was named after Giocchino Rossini, composer and gourmet. He was equaly well-known as a prolific opera composer and lover of good food and came from Pesaro in the Marche. Tagliatelle (home-made, of course) can be used instead of spaghetti. It may not be as Rossini liked it, but it is still very good indeed.

Bring a large saucepan of lightly salted water to the boil and cook the spaghetti until al dente and drain.

Melt the butter in a frying pan with a good pinch of freshly ground black pepper. Swirl the pan around gently for a few minutes to allow the flavours to combine, add the drained pasta and coat well with the butter. Serve with shaved truffle and freshly grated Parmesan.

Frittata di Maccheroni

Pasta Omelette

Jokes are often made about the Neapolitans' love of pasta frittatas – 'Those poor people of Naples! Their cuisine is so limited they even put pasta in their omelettes!' Of course, the Neopolitans don't take to this teasing too kindly. They consider their pasta frittatas a stroke of genius.

All you need for this dish are eggs, left-over pasta and its sauce, parsley, cheese and a desperate hunger. It is so quick and easy. Double or triple the other ingredients, according to how much pasta you have.

Mix the pasta, egg, cheese and parsley together.

Heat a non-stick frying pan and tip in the pasta mixture. Press down with the back of a spoon to make a flat cake. Cook on both sides until golden, as for a flat omelette. Serve immediately.

400g (14oz) pasta with its sauce (Linguine con le Lenticchie works well – page 121)

2 eggs

2 tablespoons freshly grated Parmesan or pecorino cheese

2 tablespoons finely chopped fresh parsley

serves 4

(V)

Frittata di Spaghettini e Asparagi

Pasta Omelette with Asparagus

400g (14oz) asparagus

1 tablespoon extra virgin olive oil

75g (3oz) unsmoked pancetta, thinly sliced and cut into large julienne strips

200g (7oz) Asiago cheese, diced

salt and freshly ground black pepper

150g (5oz) spaghettini

3 eggs

40g (1½oz) Parmesan cheese, freshly grated

butter, for greasing

serves 4–6

Wash the asparagus thoroughly and trim the stems, removing the tough ends. Cut the asparagus into 3cm (1¼in) lengths.

Bring a saucepan of lightly salted water to the boil, cook the asparagus for 2 minutes and drain.

Heat the oil in a frying pan and quickly fry the pancetta. Drain and place in a bowl with the asparagus and Asiago cheese.

Bring a large saucepan of lightly salted water to the boil, cook the spaghettini until al dente and drain.

Add the spaghettini to the asparagus, pancetta and Asiago cheese mixture. Mix well together. Preheat the oven to 200°C/400°F/gas mark 6.

Beat the eggs with the Parmesan and salt and pepper to taste. Add the egg mixture to the spaghettini and asparagus mixture and mix well with a fork.

Butter a 23cm (9in) round non-stick gratin dish. Place the spaghettini mixture in the dish and cook in the oven for 15 minutes.

Turn out on to a large, warmed plate and serve cut into wedges.

Bigoli coi Rovinassi

Bigoli with Chicken Liver Sauce

This recipe originates from Venice, although bigoli are also a speciality of Mantova. In Mantova the expression '*andare a bigoli*' (going for bigoli), means 'to go out for an important dinner'. *Rovinassi* is Venetian dialect for chicken livers. The sauce for this recipe is very easy and quick to make and the result is very tasty.

Make the pasta and knead for 10 minutes (page 10). Pass through a spaghetti cutting machine, or pass through the tagliatelle blades on a pasta machine, set at no. 4. (In north-eastern Italy, a special cutting machine called a *torchio* is used for making bigoli.) Leave the pasta to rest for 1 hour before boiling.

Bring a large saucepan of lightly salted water to the boil, cook the bigoli until al dente.

While the pasta is cooking, **make the sauce**. Melt the butter with the olive oil in a frying pan. When the mixture is foaming, add the garlic and sage and sauté until the garlic is golden. Add the chicken livers and sauté briskly for 1–2 minutes.

Pour the Marsala and white wine over the livers and cook briskly until the mixture becomes glazed. Season with salt and pepper to taste.

Pour the chicken liver sauce over the drained bigoli and sprinkle with Parmesan. Serve immediately.

FOR THE BIGOLI

250g (9oz) wholemeal flour

75g (3oz) plain white flour

4 large eggs

salt

OR 350g (12oz) wholemeal spaghetti

FOR THE SAUCE

75g (3oz) butter

4 tablespoons extra virgin olive oil

2 garlic cloves, finely chopped

4 teaspoons finely chopped fresh sage leaves

350g (12oz) chicken livers, cleaned and cut into small pieces

4 tablespoons Marsala

4 tablespoons dry white wine

salt and freshly ground black pepper

freshly grated Parmesan cheese

serves 4–6

(V)

Spaghetti ai Frutti di Mare al Cartoccio

Spaghetti with Seafood in a Parcel

Pasta cooked *al cartoccio* is a modern invention.

Wash the shellfish well under cold running water, soak in salted water for about 2 hours and drain.

Wash the prawns and Dublin Bay prawns under cold running water.

Heat the oil in a large saucepan, add the chilli flakes, shallot, garlic and all the seafood and cook for 3 minutes. Add the tomatoes and herbs and cook, stirring occasionally, for a further 5 minutes. Season with salt and pepper.

Meanwhile, bring a large pan of lightly salted water to the boil and cook the spaghetti until al dente.

Preheat the oven to 230°C/450°F/gas mark 8.

Drain the pasta, add to the seafood mixture and toss for 2 minutes.

Prepare four large sheets of cooking parchment or foil. Divide the pasta and sauce between the sheets and fold up, sealing well to make secure parcels. Place the parcels on a baking tray and cook in the oven for 5 minutes or until the paper has puffed up.

Serve each diner with his or her own parcel to open individually.

350g (12oz) shellfish, including mussels and Venus clams

salt and freshly ground black pepper

8 Dublin Bay prawns

20 prawns

6 tablespoons extra virgin olive oil

pinch of chilli flakes

1 shallot, finely chopped

1 garlic clove, finely chopped

6 plum tomatoes, peeled, seeded and diced

8 fresh basil leaves, shredded

1 tablespoon finely chopped fresh parsley

250g (9oz) spaghetti

serves 4

Cestini di Spaghetti con Frutti di Mare

Seafood in Spaghetti Baskets

FOR THE SPAGHETTI BASKETS

salt

250g (9oz) spaghetti

2 tablespoons extra virgin olive oil

olive oil for deep-frying

FOR THE SEAFOOD

400g (14oz) squid

400g (14oz) raw king prawns

400g (14oz) fresh mussels

6 tablespoons extra virgin olive oil

1 garlic clove, finely chopped

1 tablespoon chopped fresh parsley

salt and freshly ground black pepper

5 tablespoons dry white wine

50g (2oz) butter, diced

serves 6

Bring a large saucepan of lightly salted water to the boil. Break up the spaghetti and cook until al dente. Drain, dress with the extra virgin olive oil and leave to go cold.

To prepare the seafood, wash and skin the squid. Remove the ink sacs and heads. Cut off and reserve the tentacles and discard the rest of the heads and the ink sacs. Remove and discard the quill and cut the bodies into rings. Set aside with the tentacles.

Peel the prawns and remove and discard the intestinal veins.

Scrub the mussels well under cold running water and remove any beards. Discard mussels that have cracked shells or that do not close when tapped.

Put the cleaned mussels in a large pan with 2 tablespoons of the olive oil. Cover and cook, shaking the pan occasionally, until the shells open. Discard any that have not opened. Remove the mussels from the shells, discarding any that remain stubbornly closed, strain the cooking liquid and reserve.

Heat the oil for deep-frying. Meanwhile, divide the cold spaghetti into 12 heaps. Put a heap of spaghetti into a potato-nest fryer and clip the inner basket in place. Deep-fry the spaghetti nest until golden. Lift out of the oil and remove gently from the basket. Drain on kitchen paper.

Repeat until all the spaghetti has been used to make 12 baskets.

Heat 2 tablespoons of the remaining olive oil in a pan and fry the prawns with the garlic for 3–4 minutes.

Heat the remaining olive oil in another pan and fry the squid for 3–4 minutes Add the prawns, mussels and parsley and season with salt and pepper.

Using a slotted spoon, divide the seafood between the spaghetti baskets. Keep warm.

Add the reserved mussel cooking liquid and white wine to the seafood cooking juices and boil to reduce to a sauce. Add the butter and cook gently for a further 2 minutes. Pour the sauce over the seafood and serve.

TAGLIATELLE

05

Tagliatelle, an egg and flour pasta that takes its name from the word *tagliato*, to cut, comes in either dried or fresh form. It originates from the Pianura Padana area, the Po valley in the north of Italy – especially in Emilia. In Italy there is no such dish as spaghetti bolognese; it is tagliatelle bolognese. The combination of Neapolitan pasta with Bolognese sauce seems to be an American or British invention. Under the heading tagliatelle, we also include tagliolini (thinner than tagliatelle), pappardelle (a wider version) and fettuccine (the Roman version) – not forgetting trenette, from Liguria, which derives its name from the Genovese dialect word *trena* that means little string.

Trenette alla Barba di Frate e Prosciutto

Trenette with Barba di Frate and Parma Ham

200g (7oz) *barba di frate* or spinach

4 tablespoons extra virgin olive oil

1 small onion, finely chopped

50g (2oz) Parma ham, cut in julienne strips

salt and freshly ground black pepper

300g (10½oz) fresh trenette

Parmesan cheese shavings, to garnish

serves 4

Barba di frate, also known as *roscani* in the Marche and *agretto* in Lazio, is an unusual vegetable which has chive-like leaves and a slightly acid taste, quite similar to spinach. It is a member of the spinach and beetroot family and is considered a delicacy. *Barba di frate* is good dressed with extra virgin olive oil, garlic and chopped mint, and served with hard-boiled eggs and fresh sardines cooked on a barbecue. Never cover *barba di frate* when cooking or it will go black.

For a vegetarian option, replace the Parma ham with sun-dried tomatoes cut into julienne strips.

To make the pasta by hand, follow the instructions on page 10, or purchase fresh.

To prepare the *barba di frate*, remove the woody part and wash thoroughly to remove all the soil.

Heat the olive oil in a large saucepan and fry the onion until soft. Add the Parma ham and cook for a few more minutes. Remove from the heat and keep warm.

Bring a large pan of lightly salted water to the boil and cook the trenette with the *barba di frate* until the pasta is al dente. Drain and add to the Parma ham mixture. Toss over a high heat for a few minutes, then season with pepper.

Turn into a large, warmed serving dish, scatter over shavings of Parmesan and serve immediately.

Linguine con le Lenticchie

Linguine with Lentil Sauce

The famous lentils, *lenticchie di Castelluccio*, come from the plain of Castelluccio in Umbria. Castelluccio is in the National park of the Sibillini mountains and is 1,500 feet above sea level; the climate and terrain are perfect for the production of lentils. The great advantage of these lentils is that they do not need soaking.

Lentils are much used in Italy during the Lenten period, as well as being obligatory for New Year's Eve, the feast day of San Silvestro. They are supposed to represent wealth – perhaps because they look like money or maybe for their nutritive value, which has been held in great esteem since the time of ancient civilisations. This is a typical dish from Campania.

To make the pasta by hand, follow the instructions on page 10, or purchase fresh.

Heat 4 tablespoons of the olive oil in a saucepan and fry the onion, carrot, celery and garlic until soft.

Add the lentils and stir in for 1–2 minutes, then add the wine and allow to evaporate. Stir in the passata. Gently cook for about 30 minutes or until the lentils are tender. (The cooking time depends on the age of the lentils.) Season the sauce with salt and keep warm.

Bring a large saucepan of lightly salted water to the boil and cook the pasta until al dente.

Meanwhile, heat the remaining olive oil in a small pan and add the chilli.

Drain the pasta and tip into a large, warmed serving dish. Add the chilli oil and toss to coat. Pour the lentil sauce over the pasta, stir well and serve immediately with freshly grated Parmesan.

---

6 tablespoons extra virgin olive oil

1 small onion, finely chopped

1 small carrot, finely chopped

½ celery stick, finely chopped

1 garlic clove, finely chopped

100g (3½oz) dried lentils, preferably Castelluccio

5 tablespoons dry white wine

200ml (7fl oz) fresh Passata (page 15) or shop-bought. If using thick passata, add an equal amount of water.

salt

400g (14oz) fresh linguine or trenette

½ small fresh red chilli, finely chopped

freshly grated Parmesan cheese, to serve

serves 8–10

Ⓥ

Trenette al Pesto

Trenette with Pesto

50 large fresh basil leaves

25g (1oz) pine nuts

2 garlic cloves, peeled

good pinch of salt

100g (3½oz) freshly grated
Parmesan cheese

about 125ml (4fl oz) extra virgin
olive oil

100g (3½oz) small French beans,
trimmed

3 potatoes, peeled and diced

600g (1¼lb) fresh trenette

serves 6

Round Recce and Camogli in Liguria, French beans and potatoes are cooked with the trenette. If you use trofie or pennete rigate instead of trenette, this dish may be served cold with shavings of mature pecorino or Parmesan cheese.

To make the pasta by hand, follow the instructions on page 10, or purchase fresh.

Wash and carefully dry the basil leaves. Combine the basil leaves, pine nuts, garlic, salt and Parmesan in a blender. Blend in enough olive oil to obtain a smooth sauce. Alternatively, pound together the basil, pine nuts, garlic and salt in a mortar with a pestle, then gradually work in the cheese, followed by the oil. Set aside at room temperature.

Place the beans and potatoes in a large saucepan of salted water and bring to the boil. When they are almost cooked, add the trenette and cook until al dente.

Drain the pasta and vegetables, but not too thoroughly, and put in a warmed bowl. Add the pesto and fold in. Serve immediately.

Ⓥ

Tagliatelle con Salsa di Fagioli e Salsicce

Tagliatelle with Bean and Sausage Sauce

175g (6oz) dry borlotti beans, soaked overnight in cold water

175ml (6fl oz) extra virgin olive oil

100g (3½oz) sausage meat

150g (5oz) Parma ham

100g (3½oz) finely chopped celery

100g (3½oz) finely chopped carrot

100g (3½oz) finely chopped onion

2 garlic cloves, finely chopped

1kg (2¼lb) tomatoes, peeled, seeded and finely chopped

salt

passata, if necessary, (page 15)

800g (1¾lb) fresh tagliatelle

freshly grated Parmesan cheese, to serve

serves 8

This recipe comes from the spectacular mountain area of the Marche, the Sibillini area. It is a winter dish, which we have eaten there many times when we have stopped for a quick bite. It certainly warms you up.

The mountain range takes its name from Sybils, the prophetesses of classical mythology, who hid here in the *Grotto delle Fate* (Cave of Furies) when she was chased out of the underworld. Pontius Pilate is believed to have been buried here on a high tarn called *Lago di Pilato*.

To make the pasta by hand, follow the instructions on page 10, or purchase fresh.

Drain the beans and place in a large saucepan. Cover with unsalted water, bring to the boil and cook for about 1 hour or until tender. (The cooking time depends on the age of the beans.)

Heat the olive oil in a pan and fry the sausage meat and Parma ham for 1–2 minutes. Add the celery, carrot, onion and garlic, and fry until soft.

Add the tomatoes, lower the heat and cook gently for 30 minutes.

Drain the beans, add to the tomato sauce and cook for a further 15 minutes. Some of the beans will break up and thicken the sauce. If the sauce needs a little thinning, add the passata.

Meanwhile, bring a large pan of lightly salted water to the boil and cook the tagliatelle until al dente, then drain and tip into a warmed serving bowl. Add the sauce and toss well to mix. Serve immediately with grated Parmesan cheese.

Involtini di Melanzane con Tagliolini

Aubergine Rolls Stuffed with Tagliolini

To make the pasta by hand, follow the instructions on page 10, or purchase fresh.

Bring a large saucepan of lightly salted water or stock to the boil and cook the tagliolini until al dente.

Meanwhile, brush the sliced aubergines with olive oil and grill on a ridged grill pan. Remove from the pan and dry on absorbent kitchen paper.

Drain the pasta and mix it with half the passata, one-third of the pecorino and all the mozzarella and mix well.

Preheat the oven to 200°C/400°F/gas mark 6.

Divide the pasta between the aubergine slices, placing it centrally on each one, and fold the ends of the aubergine over the pasta to make a roll.

Spoon a layer of the remaining passata into a gratin dish large enough to hold the aubergine rolls in a single layer. Place the aubergine rolls in the dish and cover with the remaining passata. Sprinkle with the remaining pecorino and bake for about 15 minutes. Serve immediately.

Salt

2.5 litres (4½ pints) vegetable stock or water

250g (9oz) fresh tagliolini

3 tablespoons extra virgin olive oil

3 medium aubergines, thinly sliced lengthways

500ml (18fl oz) fresh Passata (page 15) or shop-bought, flavoured with 20 shredded fresh basil leaves

100g (3½oz) freshly grated pecorino cheese

110g (4oz) mozzarella cheese, finely diced

serves 4–6

(V)

Tagliolini con Carciofi e Prosciutto

Tagliolini with Artichokes and Parma Ham

juice of 1 lemon

4 purple artichokes (see introduction)

4 tablespoons extra virgin olive oil

50g (2oz) Parma ham, cut in julienne strips

2 large spring onions, trimmed and chopped

5 tablespoons dry white wine

5 tablespoons water

salt and freshly ground black pepper

400g (14oz) fresh tagliolini

chopped fresh flat leaf parsley, to garnish

Parmesan cheese shavings, to garnish

serves 4

Use the viola or violetti variety of globe artichokes for this dish. These are small, young, and have no hairy chokes (or very little), so once the outer leaves are removed, the whole artichoke can be eaten. Although we have suggested using Parma ham here, in the Marche *prosciutto di Carpegna* or *prosciutto nostrano* would be used. These are available from good Italian delicatessens.

To make the pasta by hand, follow the instructions on page 10, or purchase fresh.

Preheat the oven to 200°C/400° F/gas mark 6. Have ready a large bowl of cold water to which the lemon juice has been added.

Wash and trim the artichokes, and remove the hard outer leaves. If the tops of the remaining leaves are hard, trim off approximately 2.5cm (1in) Cut each artichoke lengthways into six and drop into the bowl of acidulated water.

Heat the olive oil in a small flameproof casserole and fry the ham and spring onions for 1–2 minutes.

Drain the artichokes, add them to the pan and cook over a moderate heat, stirring frequently, for 10 minutes.

Add the wine and allow to evaporate. Add the water, then cover the casserole and transfer to the oven. Cook for about 20 minutes or until the sauce is reduced and the artichokes are tender. Season with salt and pepper. (The sauce can be prepared in advance and then reheated for serving).

Meanwhile, bring a large saucepan of lightly salted water to the boil and cook the tagliolini until al dente. Drain and tip into a large, warmed serving dish. Pour the sauce over the pasta, scatter over the parsley and Parmesan shavings and serve immediately.

Linguine Verdi con Carciofi

Green Linguine with Artichokes

juice of 1 lemon

4 purple artichokes

4 tablespoons extra virgin olive oil

1 garlic clove, peeled

25–50ml (1–2fl oz) hot water (optional)

salt and freshly ground black pepper

5 plum tomatoes, peeled, seeded and diced

1 tablespoon finely chopped fresh parsley

200g (7oz) fresh peas

250g (9oz) dried linguine verdi

60g (1½oz) freshly grated Parmesan cheese

FOR THE BÉCHAMEL SAUCE

30g (1¼oz) tablespoons butter

20g (¾oz) flour

400ml (14fl oz) milk, warmed

salt

pinch of grated nutmeg

serves 4–6

Guiseppe Verdi's wife once wrote from Russia, 'It would take really perfect tagliatelle and maccheroni to put him in a good mood, amidst all this ice and all these fur coats!'

To make the pasta by hand, follow the instructions on page 10, or purchase fresh.

Have ready a large bowl of cold water to which the lemon juice has been added. Cut the stalks off the artichokes and remove the tough outer leaves. Cut the artichokes in half, remove the chokes and slice. Immediately drop them into the bowl of acidulated water. Heat the olive oil in a large saucepan. Drain the artichoke slices and add to the pan with the garlic. Cover and cook over a very low heat for 10 minutes, adding a little hot water if necessary.

Season with salt and freshly ground black pepper. Add the tomatoes and parsley and cook for a further 5 minutes.

Preheat the oven to 180°C/350°F/gas mark 4.

Meanwhile, make the béchamel sauce and stir in 20g (¾oz) of the Parmesan.

Bring a large saucepan of lightly salted water to the boil. Add the peas, bring back to the boil and cook. Add the linguine and cook until al dente.

Drain the peas and pasta, tip into a large bowl, add the béchamel sauce and the artichokes, and mix well together.

Transfer to a large gratin dish, sprinkle with the remaining Parmesan and bake for 20 minutes. Serve immediately.

Ⓥ

Tagliatelle con Salsa di Baccala

Tagliatelle with Salt Cod Sauce

In Italy, the Venetians and Genoese were the first to use salt cod, followed by the Neapolitans and Sicilians, but it was rarely eaten by the noble class. Bartolomeo Scappi, cook to Pius V, mentioned baccala in his cook book in 1570, then there was no word of it for two hundred years. Another dish originally served on fasting days, it was always considered food for the working classes. Nowadays it is considered a delicacy.

To make the pasta by hand, follow the instructions on page 10, or purchase fresh.

First, desalt the cod for the filling. Wash it well under cold running water, then place in a colander, skin side up, and soak in a large bowl of cold water for 3 days, changing the water regularly times. The fish must be submerged all the time.

Heat the olive oil in a saucepan and gently fry the garlic and onion. Pour in the wine, bring to the boil and allow it to bubble fiercely for a few minutes.

Reduce the heat, add the tomato coulis and the tomato purée and stir in well. Bring the sauce to the boil and add the cod. Reduce the heat and simmer gently for 1 hour.

Stir in the anchovies and season with a generous sprinkling of black pepper.

Bring a large saucepan of lightly salted water to the boil and cook the tagliatelle until al dente.

Drain and turn into a large, warmed serving dish. Pour over the sauce, sprinkle with the parsley and serve immediately.

6 tablespoons extra virgin olive oil

12 garlic cloves, finely chopped

½ onion, finely chopped

175ml (6fl oz) white wine

1.5 litres (2½ pints) tomato coulis

1 tablespoon tomato purée

500g (18oz) salt cod, soaked, boned and cut into 2cm (1in) cubes. Left-over scraps of salt cod can be used for this dish.

8 anchovy fillets, finely mashed

freshly ground black pepper

400g (14oz) fresh tagliatelle

finely chopped fresh parsley, to garnish

serves 4

Jack

Our seven-year-old grandson, Jack, knows his food very well and one evening when we took him to a nearby restaurant, he decided that, as he had not had Tagliatelle Bolognese for a long time, he would go for that. We could see the look of expectancy in his eyes. The tagliatelle arrived, he tasted it and very sadly said, 'Not as good as Anna's'. Anna was one of our Italian staff who made Bolognese ragù for his mother when she was small and now made it for him. Hers is the tops. Later on, an ice cream arrived for him. I asked, 'How is that Jack?' Very, very mournfully, he replied, 'Not as good as Anna's'. Anna is also the Queen of ice cream making.

Tagliatelle con Sugo di Anitra

Tagliatelle with Duck Sauce

400g (14oz) fresh tagliatelle (page 10)

freshly grated Parmesan cheese, to serve

FOR THE SAUCE

4 tablespoons extra virgin olive oil

3 duck legs

4 slices pancetta, finely chopped

½ onion, finely chopped

1 garlic clove, finely chopped

1 carrot, finely chopped

1 celery stick, finely chopped

2 fresh parsley sprigs

2 fresh marjoram sprigs

1 bay leaf

salt and freshly ground black pepper

5 tablespoons dry white wine

500g (18oz) tomatoes, peeled, seeded and diced

2 tablespoons tomato purée

serves 4

This duck recipe is most common in central Italy. Duck was always served, in one form or another, during the periods of sowing and harvesting. It was traditionally given to the hired hands. This sauce can also be served with potato gnocchi.

To make the pasta by hand, follow the instructions on page 10, or purchase fresh.

To make the sauce, heat 2 tablespoons of the olive oil in a frying pan and cook the duck legs until golden all over. Transfer to a flameproof casserole.

Heat the remaining oil in a clean frying pan and cook the pancetta, onion, garlic, carrot and celery until soft. Add to the duck legs with the herbs and season with salt and pepper.

Add the wine and cook over a high heat until reduced. Add the diced tomatoes and tomato purée, stir and cook for a few minutes.

Pour in just enough water to cover the ingredients. Cover and simmer gently for 45–60 minutes or until the duck is tender.

Remove the duck from the casserole, take the meat from the bones and dice finely. Skim off any fat from the sauce and remove and discard the herbs. Return the duck meat to the sauce and check the seasoning.

Meanwhile, bring a large saucepan of lightly salted water to the boil and cook the tagliatelle until al dente.

Drain the pasta and tip into a large, warmed serving dish. Pour over the duck sauce and sprinkle with Parmesan. Serve immediately.

Tagliatelle Verde con Piselli

Green Tagliatelle with Peas

40g (1½oz) butter

40g (1½oz) pancetta cut in
julienne strips

1 tablespoon finely chopped
onion

150g (5oz) shelled peas

125ml (4fl oz) vegetable stock
or water

salt and freshly ground
black pepper

1 tablespoon milk

1 tablespoon chopped
fresh chives

1 egg mixed with 2 tablespoons
freshly grated Parmesan cheese

400g (14oz) fresh green tagliatelle

serves 10

To make the pasta by hand, follow the instructions on page 10, or purchase fresh.

Heat the butter in a frying pan, add the pancetta and onion and cook over a gentle heat. Add the peas and stock or water and season with pepper. Bring to the boil, lower the heat, and simmer until the peas are cooked. Check the seasoning – the pancetta may be very salty – and add salt if necessary.

Put the milk, chives and the egg and Parmesan mixture into a large saucepan and mix well. Set aside.

Bring a large saucepan of lightly salted water to the boil and cook the tagliatelle until al dente. Drain and add to the egg and Parmesan mixture. Mix well.

Pour over the pea sauce and stir in over a low heat. Turn into a large, warmed serving dish and serve immediately. Do not add more Parmesan when serving – it will only dry it out.

Tagliatelle con Ragù di Coniglio

Tagliatelle with Rabbit Sauce

Tagliatelle, a ribbon-shaped pasta, was invented by Mastro Zafirano, who was cook to Conte Benvoglio when Lucrezia Borgia married Duke d'Este in 1487. The tagliatelle are supposed to represent Lucrezia's long blonde tresses. The exact width for tagliatelle – 1.5cm (⅗in) – is registered in the chamber of commerce in Bologna.

To make the pasta by hand, follow the instructions on page 10, or purchase fresh.

For the ragù, heat 4 tablespoons of the olive oil in a frying pan and cook the pancetta briefly. Add the onion, carrot, celery and garlic and cook until they are soft and golden. Using a slotted spoon, transfer the pancetta and vegetables to a heavy, flameproof casserole.

Heat the remaining oil in the frying pan and fry the rabbit pieces until golden on all sides. Transfer to the casserole.

Add the rosemary, bouquet garni, parsley, passata and wine to the casserole and gradually bring to the boil. Add just enough hot water to cover the rabbit joints and season with salt and pepper. Reduce the heat, cover and cook gently for 1 hour or until the rabbit is tender. (If the rabbit is farmed, the cooking time may be shorter.)

Remove the rabbit joints from the sauce as they are ready (different joints require different cooking times), cut the meat off the bone and dice. Return the diced meat to the sauce. Remove and discard the herbs and check the seasoning. The sauce should be quite thick, so boil to reduce, if necessary.

Bring a large saucepan of lightly salted water to the boil and cook the pasta until al dente. Drain and turn into a large, warm serving dish. Pour over the rabbit sauce, sprinkle with Parmesan and serve immediately.

600g (1¼lb) fresh tagliatelle or pappardelle

freshly grated Parmesan cheese

FOR THE RAGÙ

6 tablespoons extra virgin olive oil

100g (3½oz) pancetta, diced

60g (2½oz) onion, finely chopped

60g (2½oz) carrot, finely chopped

60g (2½oz) celery, finely diced

2 garlic cloves, finely chopped

800g (1¾lb) rabbit joints, preferably the hind legs

2 fresh rosemary sprigs, tied in a square of muslin

1 bouquet garni

1 bunch of fresh parsley

240ml (8fl oz) fresh Passata (page 15) or shop-bought

5 tablespoons dry white wine

salt and freshly ground black pepper

serves 6

Pappardelle con Capesante e Salsa di Pesto

Pappardelle with Scallops and Pesto

1 quantity Basic Pasta Dough
(page 10)

FOR THE PESTO
20 fresh basil leaves
20 fresh flat-leaf parsley leaves
3 garlic cloves
50g (2oz) pine nuts
175ml (6fl oz) extra virgin olive oil
salt and freshly ground
black pepper

FOR THE SCALLOPS
2 tablespoons extra virgin olive oil
200g (7oz) small scallops or large
ones cut in half
salt and pepper
4 tablespoons tomato peeled,
seeded and diced
24 small fresh dill sprigs

serves 4

A Ligurian recipe combining the much-loved pesto with scallops.
Basil, so beloved by the Ligurians, grows easily in Liguria – it loves the temperate rainy climate. The plant originates from the Orient and obviously came to Genoa via its maritime contacts. There is a legend that basil first grew in the pot where Salome buried the head of St John the Baptist. Another legend says that the Empress Elena, mother of the Roman Emperor Constantine, found it growing on the spot where Jesus was crucified.

To make the pasta by hand, follow the instructions on page 10, or purchase fresh.

Roll out the pasta dough and cut it into 2 x 20cm (¾ x 8in) strips with a pastry cutter.
   Place all the pesto ingredients in a food processor and process to a paste.
   For the scallops, heat the olive oil in a frying pan and sauté the scallops for 3 minutes. Season with salt and pepper, then toss the scallops with 2 tablespoons of the pesto.
   Bring a large saucepan of lightly salted water to the boil and cook the pasta until al dente. Drain and toss with the scallops and pesto. Serve immediately, garnished with the diced tomato and dill sprigs.

Fettuccine con Ragù di Coda alla Vaccinara

Fettuccine with Oxtail Sauce

4 tablespoons extra virgin olive oil

1 large oxtail cut in pieces

1 celery stick, finely chopped

1 carrot, finely chopped

1 small onion, finely chopped

2 garlic cloves, finely chopped

400ml (14fl oz) fresh Passata (page 15) or shop-bought

1 tablespoon tomato purée

1 bay leaf

salt and freshly ground black pepper

good pinch of ground cloves

400g (14oz) fettuccine (tagliatelle)

serves 4

This recipe originated in Rome in a restaurant called Checchino. It originally contained chocolate and pine nuts, as well as the ingredients given here. Checchino's became famous for their dishes using cheap cuts of meat. The word *vaccinara* is Roman dialect for butcher and *coda alla vaccinara* has now become a symbol of Roman cooking. *Fettuccine* is a Roman dialect word for Tagliatelle.

To make the pasta by hand, follow the instructions on page 10, or purchase fresh.

Heat the olive oil in a frying pan and cook the oxtail until golden all over.

Add the vegetables, passata, tomato purée and bay leaf, then pour in just enough boiling water to cover the oxtail. Season with salt and pepper.

Cook gently for 2 hours, adding the ground cloves halfway through the cooking time. If the sauce reduces too much, add more boiling water.

Remove the pieces of oxtail when nearly done. Cut the meat from the bone and chop. Return the meat to the pan and cook for a further 30 minutes.

Bring a large saucepan of lightly salted water to the boil and cook the fettuccine until al dente. Drain and turn into a large, warmed bowl. Pour on the sauce and mix well. Serve immediately. Parmesan is not usually served with this sauce as it is already quite rich.

Ⓥ

Pappardelle con Sugo di Lepre

Wide Ribbon Noodles with Hare Sauce

This recipe is from the mountainous regions of Tuscany, which is well known for its game. Pappardelle are strips of pasta cut with a pastry cutter from a whole sheet. The strips should be 10–20cm (4–8in) long by 2–3cm (¾–1¼in) wide.

To make the pasta by hand, follow the instructions on page 10, or purchase fresh.

Place the hare portions in a large, non-metallic dish in a single layer. Pour in sufficient wine to cover and add 1 of the bouquets garni. Cover and marinate for at least 24 hours.

Heat 3 tablespoons of the olive oil in a frying pan. Add the onion, celery, garlic and bacon and fry until golden. Using a slotted spoon, transfer to a flameproof casserole. Remove and discard the bouquet garni from the marinade. Drain the hare portions, pat dry with kitchen paper and dust with flour. Reserve the marinade.

Add the remaining olive oil to the frying pan, reheat and fry the hare portions until sealed on all sides. Transfer to the casserole.

Heat the reserved marinade in a pan and pour over the hare. Add the remaining bouquet garni and season with salt and pepper. Cover the casserole and cook over a low heat for 1 hour or until the hare is tender. (The cooking time depends on the age of the hare.)

Remove the hare portions from the casserole and cut the meat from the bone. Dice the meat and return it to the sauce. Check the seasoning.

Bring a large saucepan of lightly salted water to the boil and cook the pappardelle until al dente. Drain and turn into a large, warmed serving dish. Pour on the sauce and sprinkle with Parmesan. Serve immediately.

1 hare, cut into portions

about ½ bottle red wine

2 bouquets garni, consisting of 2–3 fresh parsley sprigs, 1–2 bay leaves, 1 fresh thyme sprig, 1 fresh sage sprig and 2 fresh rosemary sprigs tied together

7 tablespoons extra virgin olive oil

1 onion, finely chopped

1 celery stick, finely chopped

1 garlic clove, finely chopped

50g (2oz) bacon, diced

flour, for dusting

salt and freshly ground black pepper

600g (1¼lb) fresh pappardelle

freshly grated Parmesan cheese

serves 6–8

Bracioline con Salsa di Pomodoro e Tagliatelle

Steak Rolls with Tomato Sauce and Tagliatelle

12 slices chuck steak, weighing 60g (2oz) each

12 streaky bacon slices

bunch of fresh parsley, finely chopped

2 tablespoons dried oregano

3 garlic cloves, finely chopped

50g (2oz) pine nuts

100g (3½oz) freshly grated Parmesan cheese

salt and fresh coarsely ground black pepper

4 tablespoons olive oil

1.1kg (2¼lb) plum tomatoes, peeled and finely chopped

350ml (12fl oz) dry white wine

4 tablespoons tomato purée, mixed with 2 tablespoons hot water

bouquet garni, consisting of a celery stick, 1 bay leaf and 2–3 fresh parsley sprigs tied together

400g (14oz) fresh tagliatelle

serves 4

A few of the women who first worked for us at our restaurant The Walnut Tree Inn came from the south of Italy. Maria, one of these ladies, loved making this recipe, which was her own. Originally, this dish was made with horsemeat and was always served at weddings or special festivals. Needless to say, we always made it with beef.

To make the pasta by hand, follow the instructions on page 10, or purchase fresh.

Pound the slices of beef between 2 sheets of greaseproof paper. Put a slice of bacon on each piece of meat. Sprinkle over the parsley, oregano and garlic and divide the pine nuts and Parmesan cheese between the pieces of meat. Season with salt and pepper, fold in the sides slightly, then roll up the pieces of steak and secure with a cocktail stick.

Heat the olive oil in a heavy, flameproof casserole and fry the rolls until brown all over. Add the tomatoes, white wine and diluted tomato purée and reduce the heat. Make sure the beef rolls are covered with sauce. Season lightly and add the bouquet garni, then simmer very gently, stirring frequently, for 2 hours. Add a little boiling water to prevent the sauce from catching on the base of the casserole, if necessary. Do not allow the sauce to boil or the meat will toughen – a gentle ripple must be maintained.

Check the meat after 2 hours, as it may need longer cooking. Adjust the seasoning if necessary. Remove and discard the cocktail sticks.

Bring a large saucepan of lightly salted water to the boil and cook the pasta until al dente. Turn into a large, warmed serving dish, mix in the sauce and top with the beef rolls. Serve immediately.

Tagliolini con Sugo d'Agnello

Tagliolini with Lamb Sauce

6 tablespoons olive oil

600g (1¼lb) boneless lean lamb, finely diced

1 onion, finely chopped

2 garlic cloves, finely chopped

450g (1lb) plum tomatoes, peeled and finely chopped

2 fresh red chillies, seeded and finely chopped

salt and freshly ground black pepper

pinch of chilli flakes

175ml (6fl oz) dry white wine

4 tablespoons water

2 tablespoons finely chopped fresh parsley

450g (1lb) fresh tagliolini or buy dry tagliolini

freshly grated pecorino cheese, to garnish

serves 4

This recipe comes from the austere mountainous region of the Abruzzi, just south of the Marche, where lamb is plentiful. It is almost unknown in the other regions of Italy for lamb to be used in a sauce. In the Abruzzi area, the pasta served with this sauce would be maccheroni alla chitarra. The nooodles are cut into very thin strips on a 'guitar', a rectangular frame strung with a large number of wires. Tagliolini are the closest substitute.

To make the pasta by hand, follow the instructions on page 10, or purchase fresh.

Heat the olive oil in a frying pan and fry the lamb until sealed all over. Remove with a slotted spoon and set aside.

Add the onion and garlic to the pan and fry until golden and soft. Stir in the tomatoes and cook briefly.

Return the lamb to the pan. Add the fresh chillies and season with salt, pepper and chilli flakes to taste. Add the white wine and water and cook for 30 minutes.

Meanwhile, bring a large saucepan of lightly salted water to the boil and cook the tagliolini until al dente. Turn into a large, warmed serving dish.

Add the parsley to the sauce and adjust the seasoning if necessary. Pour the sauce over the pasta, sprinkle with pecorino cheese and serve immediately.

Tagliatelle Nero e Bianco con Salmone Fumigato

Black and White Tagliatelle with Smoked Salmon

Smoked salmon pasta dishes are a standard St Valentine's Day dish in Italy. It can be served with plain tagliatelle if preferred, but the presentation of three colours is very attractive on the plate. Sachets of squid ink are available from some fishmongers.

Make the pasta (page 10), using all the ingredients except the squid ink. Divide the dough in half and add the squid ink to one portion. Knead the dough and roll out, then cut the sheets on the tagliatelle cutter of the pasta machine.

To make the sauce, melt the butter with the oil in a frying pan and cook the shallots very gently until softened.

Add the wine and cook until almost evaporated. Add the cream, dill and lemon juice and bring to the boil. Reduce the heat to very low.

Meanwhile, bring a large saucepan of lightly salted water to the boil and cook the tagliatelle until al dente. Drain, add to the sauce and mix well. Remove the pan from the heat, add the smoked salmon and season with salt and pepper. Garnish with dill and chives and serve immediately.

FOR THE PASTA

500g (18oz) Farina O or strong plain white flour

2 tablespoons olive oil

4 eggs

a little lukewarm water

ink from 3–4 squid, or 1 small sachet squid ink

pinch of salt

FOR THE SAUCE

40g (1½oz) butter

2 tablespoons olive oil

2 shallots, finely chopped

200ml (7fl oz) dry white wine

200ml (7fl oz) single cream

¼ teaspoon dried dill

a few drops of fresh lemon juice

125g (4½oz) smoked salmon, cut into julienne strips

salt and freshly ground black pepper

a few fresh dill sprigs, to garnish

1 tablespoon chopped fresh chives, to garnish

serves 6

Tagliatelle con Sugo alla Silana

Tagliatelle with Parma ham and Porcini Sauce

3 tablespoons extra virgin olive oil

50g (2oz) Parma ham cut into julienne strips

1 garlic clove, finely chopped

150g (5oz) porcini mushrooms, thinly sliced

400g (14oz) tomatoes, peeled, seeded, and diced

salt

4 fresh basil leaves, shredded

1 tablespoon finely chopped fresh parsley

pinch of chilli flakes

400g (14oz) fresh tagliatelle

serves 4

We were making our way to Catanzaro in Calabria when we decided to investigate the forest nearby called La Sila – no doubt spurred on by Norman Douglas' description of the pine tree, *Pino della Sila*, in his book *Old Calabria*. 'It is found over this whole country, and grows to a height of forty feet with a silver grey trunk, exhaling a delicious aromatic fragrance. In youth especially, where the soil is deep, it shoots up prim and demure as a Nuremberg toy; but in old age grows monstrous.'

Franco kept on saying how wonderful the place was and how perfect the woods would be for finding porcini. All I could think of was 'yes, but not in February!' Snow started to fall and the afternoon soon became very dark. We were low on petrol when we realised we were lost. Every small road looked the same and there was not a soul around to help us. Franco suddenly remarked after a long silence, 'I bet there are wolves in this forest!' Just as we were beginning to get really anxious, however, we found the right road.

That night we ate in a small trattoria-pizzeria in Catanzaro, where the proprietor offered us this dish. He used porcini that he had picked in autumn and preserved in olive oil. A man sitting near us had a pizza with porcini. Before he started eating, he fished a few red chillies out of his pocket. He saw me watching him and remarked, 'I always like more chilli so I always carry my own – would you like some?'

To make the pasta by hand, follow the instructions on page 10, or purchase fresh.

Heat the oil in a frying pan and briefly cook the Parma ham. Add the garlic and the mushrooms and fry rapidly. Add the tomatoes, stir and season with salt. Cover the frying pan, lower the heat and cook, stirring frequently, for 20 minutes.

Meanwhile, bring a large saucepan of lightly salted water to the boil and cook the tagliatelle until al dente.

When the sauce is cooked add the basil, parsley and chilli flakes and stir through.

Drain the pasta and turn it into a large, warmed serving dish, pour over the sauce and mix well. Serve immediately.

Pappardelle con Funghi Porcini

Pappardelle with Porcini Sauce

We have three favourite places for mushroom gathering, the most prolific being a wood in the Black Mountains. The terrain is difficult but the beauty of that wood and the baskets of porcini, chanterelles, pieds de mouton and trompettes de mort more than compensate for the aching limbs and sore back.

To make the pasta by hand, follow the instructions on page 10, or purchase fresh.

Heat the olive oil in a frying pan and cook the mushrooms. Add the garlic and parsley and fry briefly.

Add the white wine and cook over a high heat until almost evaporated. Add the stock and cook over a high heat until reduced to a glaze. Add the chopped walnuts and season with salt and pepper.

Bring a large saucepan of lightly salted water to the boil, cook the pappardelle until al dente and drain. Turn into a large, warmed serving dish. Pour over the mushroom and walnut sauce and sprinkle with pepper. Serve immediately.

2 tablespoons extra virgin olive oil

500g (18oz) fresh porcini mushrooms, sliced

1 garlic clove, finely chopped

1 bunch of fresh parsley, finely chopped

5 tablespoons dry white wine

200ml (7fl oz) vegetable or meat stock

20 walnut halves, chopped

salt and freshly ground black pepper

600g (1¼lb) fresh pappardelle

serves 4–6

Crostata di Tagliolini

Tagliolini Tart

salt

500g (18oz) fresh tagliolini

100g (3½oz) butter

100g (3½oz) Parmesan cheese, freshly grated

olive oil, for greasing

2–3 tablespoons fresh breadcrumbs

100g (3½oz) prosciutto, cut in julienne strips

315g (11oz) diced mozzarella cheese

FOR THE BÉCHAMEL SAUCE

110g (4oz) butter

75g (3oz) flour

1 litre (1¾ pints) milk, warmed

salt

FOR THE SAUCE

40g (1½oz) butter

50g (2oz) pancetta, cut in julienne strips

315g (11oz) shelled peas

3 spring onions, coarsely chopped

salt and freshly ground black pepper

serves 8

To make the pasta by hand, follow the instructions on page 10, or purchase fresh.

Make the béchamel sauce and, when cold, leave to harden in the fridge.

To make the sauce, melt the butter in a frying pan and gently fry the pancetta until golden brown.

Add the peas and spring onions, reduce the heat and add just enough hot water to cover the peas. Cook gently until the peas are tender and the liquid has evaporated. Season with pepper and add salt, if necessary, bearing in mind that the pancetta may be very salty.

Bring a large saucepan of lightly salted water to the boil and cook the tagliolini until al dente. Drain and toss immediately with the butter and almost all the Parmesan. Check the seasoning.

Preheat the oven to 180°C/350°F/gas mark 4.

Oil a 26cm (10½in) diameter loose-based cake tin and dust with fresh breadcrumbs. Spoon in half the tagliolini, followed by the pea mixture, prosciutto, mozzarella and half the béchamel, cut into slithers. Mix the remaining tagliolini with a little of the remaining béchamel and make a second layer. Scatter slivers of the rest of the béchamel and grated Parmesan on top.

Bake for 20 minutes. Leave to rest until lukewarm before serving.

PENNE

06

Penne rigate (large quills with ridges) and pennette (little quills) are tubular in shape and usually found in dried form, although occasionally fresh penne are available. It is a North Italian pasta which holds sauces very well and is the most popular of the tubular pastas. This chapter also includes dishes that use some other hollow pastas, such as bucatini – as well as shapes like fusilli and conchiglie.

Melanzane imbottite di Bucatini e Mozzarella

Aubergine stuffed with Bucatini and Mozzarella

4 Tunisino (pale purple) aubergines, weighing about 1.2kg (3lb) in total

olive oil, for deep-frying

5 tablespoons extra virgin olive oil

2 shallots, finely chopped

2 garlic cloves, finely chopped

1kg (2¼lb) tomatoes, peeled, seeded and diced, any juice reserved

4 tablespoons fresh Passata (page 15) or shop-bought

salt and freshly ground black pepper

generous pinch of dried oregano

250g (9oz) bucatini or penne

20 fresh basil leaves, torn

300g (10½oz) mozzarella cheese, diced

20g (¾oz) freshly grated Parmesan cheese

serves 4

This recipe is based on an idea from a restaurant, called Charleston in Palermo. Use the round, light purple variety of aubergine, known as Tunisino, for this dish.

Slice the stalk end off each aubergine to make a lid and reserve. Scoop out the flesh from the aubergines with a teaspoon, leaving a 1cm (½in) shell all round. Dice the scooped-out flesh.

Heat the olive oil in a large pan and deep-fry the aubergine shells and lids until tender. (Put the frying basket on top to keep the aubergines immersed in the oil.) Remove and drain on kitchen paper. To keep their shape, hang the shells upside down over glasses.

Preheat the oven to 200°C/400°F/gas mark 6.

Heat 4 tablespoons of the extra virgin olive oil in a saucepan and fry the shallots and garlic until golden. Add the diced aubergine flesh and fry until golden.

Add the tomatoes, with any juice, and the passata. Season with salt, pepper and oregano and cook until the sauce has thickened.

Meanwhile, bring a large saucepan of lightly salted water to the boil and cook the pasta until al dente. Drain and put in a bowl. Add the torn basil leaves, mozzarella and half the tomato sauce. Mix well.

Pour the remaining tomato sauce into a gratin dish large enough to hold the aubergine shells in a single layer. Fill the aubergine shells with the pasta mixture and set them upright in the dish. Drizzle the remaining extra virgin olive oil on top and sprinkle with the Parmesan.

Bake for 20 minutes. Serve immediately, with the lids on the top for decoration.

Ⓥ

Pasta cu li Sardi

Conchiglie with Sardines

This recipe comes from Palermo, Sicily, where toasted breadcrumbs are known as 'poor man's cheese'. When Sicilians eat this dish, they think it is the ultimate. In fact, when a Sicilian expects to eat well or earn some money, he says, '*Ammuccamu! Pasta cu li sardi*'. 'Let's stuff ourselves! With pasta and sardines.' Wild fennel is common from May to November, but the tops of bulb fennel can be used instead, if it is not available.

Heat the olive oil in a saucepan and fry the breadcrumbs, stirring frequently, until golden. Drain on kitchen paper.

Bring a large saucepan of lightly salted water to the boil and cook the fennel for 10 minutes. Drain thoroughly, reserving the water. Finely chop the fennel and set aside.

Heat half the extra virgin olive oil in a frying pan and cook the onions over a low heat until pale golden in colour. Add the pine nuts, currants, almonds, anchovies and saffron with its soaking water.

Heat the remaining extra virgin olive oil in a frying pan and cook 6 sardines over a medium heat until golden, turning them carefully so that they do not break up. Remove the sardines from the pan and set aside.

Fry the fennel and the remaining sardines in the same oil, mashing the sardines with a wooden spoon.

Preheat the oven to 190°C/375°F/gas mark 5.

Bring the reserved fennel water to the boil, add the bucatini and cook until al dente. Drain and put into a large bowl. Mix the onion mixture with the mashed fish and stir into the bucatini.

Tip the pasta mixture into a deep gratin dish, place the fried sardines on top and sprinkle with some of the fried breadcrumbs.

Bake for 10 minutes. Serve immediately, sprinkled with the remaining breadcrumbs. This dish is equally good served cold.

2 tablespoons olive oil

110g (4oz) fresh breadcrumbs

salt and freshly ground black pepper

2 bunches of wild fennel, trimmed and washed thoroughly

4 tablespoons extra virgin olive oil

2 small onions, finely chopped

50g (2oz) pine nuts

50g (2oz) currants, soaked in a little warm water and drained

50g (2oz) toasted slivered almonds

6 salted anchovies, washed, boned and mashed

pinch of saffron threads, soaked in a little water

10 medium-sized fresh sardines (about 700g/1½lb), cleaned, scaled and boned (page 161)

500g (1¼lb 2oz) bucatini

serves 4

Gambieri Croccanti

Prawns Wrapped in Crisp Pasta

salt and freshly ground black
pepper

75g (3oz) Campofilone
maccheroncini

400g (14oz) raw tiger prawns,
peeled and deveined

olive oil, for deep-frying

FOR THE DRESSING

4 tablespoons balsamic vinegar

4 tablespoons extra virgin olive oil

4 medium spring onions
(including the green parts),
sliced into thin rings

4 lemon wedges

serves 4

We first ate this dish at a lovely hotel, Il Fortino, at Porto Nuovo, near Ancona. The hotel was built as a fort in 1808 by Napoleon's Italian Viceroy. Along with various fish restaurants, it nestles at the base of a steep cliff. The little bay is like a secret place. Fishing boats bring all kinds of fish, caught in the crystal clear waters of the Adriatic, and restaurateurs and regulars come down to the pebble beach to buy it. At the far end of the bay, where the evergreen oaks that smother the mountain come down to the sea, stands the church of Santa Maria – a rare example of a Romanesque church, building in 1034.

Bring a saucepan of lightly salted water to the boil and cook the maccheroncini for 1 minute to soften. Drain and rinse under cold running water. Drain again and place on a clean tea towel to dry.

Season the prawns with salt and pepper, then wrap each one loosely in maccheroncini. Heat the olive oil in a deep-fryer. Fry the pasta-wrapped prawns, a few at a time, until golden all over.

Remove with a slotted spoon and drain on kitchen paper. Keep warm.

Make a dressing by mixing together the balsamic vinegar, olive oil and spring onions. Put a spoonful of the dressing in the centre of each plate, place the prawns on top and add a wedge of lemon. Serve immediately.

Reginelle con tonno e acciuge

Reginelle with tuna and anchovies

This dish is traditionally served on Christmas Eve. Do not be tempted to serve it with grated Parmesan cheese.

Heat the oil in a saucepan cook the garlic until golden. Add the tomatoes and simmer over a low heat for 10 minutes.

Add the tuna, anchovies, capers and olives and season well with pepper. Check to see if more salt is required. Stir all the ingredients into the tomato sauce to heat through, then stir in the parsley and dried chilli flakes.

Meanwhile, bring a large saucepan of lightly salted water to the boil and cook the pasta until al dente. Drain, turn into a large, warmed serving dish, pour over the sauce and mix thoroughly. Serve immediately.

4 tablespoons olive oil

2 garlic, cloves finely chopped

450g (1lb) ripe plum tomatoes, peeled, seeded and coarsely chopped

200g (7oz) can tuna in olive oil, drained and flaked

8 canned anchovy fillets, drained and chopped

1 tablespoon salt-cured capers, well washed and coarsely chopped

1½ tablespoons thinly sliced green olives

1½ tablespoons thinly sliced black olives

salt and coarsely ground black pepper

2 tablespoons finely chopped fresh parsley

pinch of dried chilli flakes

450g (1lb) reginelle, spaghetti or bucatini

serves 6

Fusilli e Fagiolini al Pomodoro con Mozzarella

Fusilli with French Beans, Tomatoes and Mozzarella

salt and freshly ground black pepper

250g (9oz) fusilli

500g (18oz) plum tomatoes

150g (5oz) cooked French beans

1 celery stick, thinly sliced, including leaves

250ml (9fl oz) fresh Passata (page 15) or shop-bought

3 tablespoons extra virgin olive oil

4 spring onions, finely chopped

1 small red chilli, seeded and thinly sliced

1 *mozzarella di bufala* (120g/ 4½oz), diced

2 fresh basil sprigs, chopped

small bunch of fresh chives, chopped

black olives (optional)

serves 4

Bring a large saucepan of lightly salted water to the boil and cook the fusilli until al dente. Drain and toss some ice cubes into the pasta to stop the cooking process. Drain again on clean tea towels.

Using a sharp knife, make a light cross at the base of each tomato. Dip the tomatoes briefly into boiling water, then remove the skins. Cut the tomatoes in half and remove the seeds. Sieve the juices from the seeds and reserve. Cut each tomato half lengthways into six.

Toss the fusilli with the beans, celery and tomato juliennes.

Put the passata, reserved tomato juices, olive oil, salt and freshly ground black pepper in a blender and process until combined. Pour the tomato mixture over the pasta and add the spring onions and chilli. Toss well.

Add the mozzarella, basil and chives and a few black olives, if liked.
Serve cold.

Ⓥ

Conchiglie all' Anconetana

Conchiglie with Sardines

Conchiglie are fairly small, shell-shaped pasta. The city of Ancona on the east coast of Italy was founded by the Greeks in 387BC. Its name comes from the ancient Greek *ancon*, elbow, because of the shape of its coastline. Ancona has a thriving shipping trade between Greece and Croatia.

Clean the sardines by first, cutting off the tail, fins and head. Remove the scales under cold running water by running your hand along the bodies from tail-end to head-end. Slit the belly and remove the guts, then push back the two sides of the sardine so that it opens up like a book, and gently remove the backbone. Trim the tiny bones away. (A friendly fishmonger will usually do this for you.)

Heat the olive oil in a frying pan and cook the garlic until golden. Add the sardines and break them up with a wooden spoon. Add the wine and allow to evaporate.

Stir in the basil and parsley and season with salt and pepper. Cook for a few seconds, then remove from the heat and keep hot.

Bring a large saucepan of lightly salted water to the boil and cook the conchiglie until al dente. Drain, tip into a large heated bowl and add the sardine sauce. Serve immediately.

300g (10½oz) fresh sardines

6 tablespoons extra virgin olive oil

1 garlic clove, finely chopped

5 tablespoons dry white wine

16–20 fresh basil leaves, torn

4 tablespoons finely chopped fresh flat leaf parsley

salt and freshly ground black pepper

275g (10oz) conchiglie

serves 6–8

Minestra di Pasta e Patate

Pasta and Potato Soup

Giacomo Leopardi (1798–1837), considered Italy's second greatest poet, is one of the few Italians who disliked pasta. He was born in Recanati, Marche, of an aristocratic family, and one can still visit the house where he was born and wander the streets of this delightful small town. To look out over the hills and sea towards Croatia and read his poem *L'Infinito* on a clear day is a breathtaking experience. Leopardi, who for a time lived in Naples, railed against the Neapolitans for eating so much pasta, saying it was probably the pasta which made them so slothful. The Neapolitans replied that if he ate more pasta he would be less of a misery! But Leopardi did not only loathe pasta. He disliked soup as well and even wrote a poem, *A Morte la Minestra* (Kill the Soup), about it. No doubt he would not have approved of this delicious and rustic recipe from Campania in the south of Italy.

Heat the oil in a frying pan and cook the bacon for 5 minutes. Add the carrot, onion and celery and cook until the onion is light golden.

Add the chilli and tomatoes and cook over a low heat, stirring frequently, for 10 minutes.

Add the potatoes and cook for a further 5 minutes. Add two-thirds of the water, cover and simmer until the potatoes are cooked.

Add the remaining water, bring to the boil and add the pasta. Stir and cook until the pasta is al dente. Add more water if necessary. Season with salt and pepper.

Remove from the heat allow to cool slightly. Serve with freshly grated Parmesan.

5 tablespoons extra virgin olive oil

110g (4oz) bacon, diced

1 carrot, diced

1 onion, diced

2 celery sticks, diced

1 whole fresh chilli

2 tomatoes, peeled, seeded and diced

500g (18oz) potatoes, peeled and diced

500ml (18fl oz) water

250g (9oz) connolicchi, or macaroncini short pasta

freshly grated Parmesan cheese, to serve

serves 6

Pasta e Fagioli

Pasta and Bean Soup

2 litres (3½ pints) water

1 fresh rosemary sprig

275g (10oz) fresh borlotti beans or 200g (7oz) dried borlotti beans, soaked for 3–4 hours, drained, then boiled vigorously for 15 minutes and drained

1 ham hock

1 onion, peeled and left whole

2 garlic cloves, peeled and left whole

2 celery sticks

2 fresh parsley sprigs

125ml (4fl oz) extra virgin olive oil, plus extra to serve

salt and freshly ground black pepper

200g (7oz) chifferi or other small tubular pasta

dried chilli flakes, to serve

serves 4

This soup is also known as *Tuone e Lampe* – Thunder and Lightning – and you can probably guess why. However, do not be put off, as it is a wonderful soup for a cold day. Although it originated in Naples, this soup has spread far and wide to other regions and is one of the dishes that competed to unite Italy.

Put the water in a heavy-based saucepan with a well-fitting lid. Tie the rosemary sprig in a piece of muslin and add to the pan with the beans, ham hock, onion, garlic, celery, parsley and olive oil. Bring to the boil, lower the heat and simmer gently for 1½ hours or until the beans are tender.

Remove rosemary and discard. Remove the ham hock, scrape the meat from the bone and dice. Remove the onion, garlic and celery and process in a blender. Pass half of the beans through a food mill or process in a blender.

Return the vegetables, diced ham and puréed beans to the soup.

Season with salt, if necessary, and freshly ground black pepper. Bring back to the boil, uncovered. Add the pasta and cook until al dente.

Serve with a dash of extra virgin olive oil and a pinch of dried chilli flakes to taste.

Fusilli con Piselli e Prosciutto

Fusilli with Peas, Parma Ham & Cream

50g (2oz) unsalted butter

200g (7oz) fresh peas

100g (3½oz) Parma ham, cut in thin strips

250ml (9fl oz) single cream

salt and freshly ground white pepper

200g (7oz) fusilli

40g (1½oz) freshly grated Parmesan cheese

serves 4

Melt the butter in a frying pan and gently cook the peas until nearly tender.

Add the ham and cream and season with salt and pepper. Cook the sauce gently until well amalgamated and creamy.

Meanwhile, bring a large saucepan of lightly salted water to the boil and cook the fusilli until al dente. Drain thoroughly, turn into a large, warmed serving dish and toss with the sauce. Sprinkle with the Parmesan and serve immediately.

Penne alla Pastora

Penne with Ricotta Cheese and Sausage

150g (5oz) *Salsicce di Maiale Marchigiani* (page 17) or other Italian sausage

2 tablespoons olive oil

275g (10oz) ridged penne

400g (14oz) ricotta cheese

salt and freshly ground black pepper

freshly grated pecorino cheese, to serve

serves 4

Pecorino Romano, the ancient cheese of the gods, is made from sheeps' milk. Columella, a first century Roman soldier and farmer, wrote a series of books called *De re Rustica*, which cover agriculture, general husbandry and farm management, and include instructions on how to make Pecorino. The cheese produced in Lazio at least 2000 years ago is made in much the same way today.

Remove the skins from the sausage and break the meat up into small pieces. Heat the olive oil in a frying pan and gently cook the sausage meat until pale gold. Do not allow it to over-brown. Remove from the pan and drain on kitchen paper.

Meanwhile, bring a large saucepan of lightly salted water to the boil and cook the penne until al dente. Drain, reserving 2–3 tablespoons of the water and leaving the pasta damp.

Sieve the ricotta cheese into a serving bowl, add the reserved pasta water and season well with pepper. Blend to a creamy paste. Add the sausage meat, drained of oil, and fold in.

Stir the pasta into the ricotta and sausage mixture. Serve immediately with grated pecorino.

Pasta al Forno Pugliese

Baked Pasta from Puglia

This Pugliese pasta dish is served on festival days.

Skin the sausages and break up the meat. Heat 2 tablespoons of olive oil in a frying pan and cook the sausage meat until light golden. Add the wine and allow to evaporate. Add the diluted tomato purée and basil leaves and season with salt and pepper to taste. Cook until the sauce is thick and flavourful.

Put one-third of the grated pecorino into a bowl and stir in the breadcrumbs, garlic and parsley. Add the minced beef and egg and mix together thoroughly. Dampen your hands and roll the mixture into cherry-size balls.

Heat the remaining olive oil in a frying pan and cook the meatballs until light golden all over. Drain on kitchen paper and add to the sausage sauce.

Meanwhile, bring a large saucepan of lightly salted water to the boil and cook the penne until al dente. Drain and set aside.

Preheat the oven to 200°C/400°F/gas mark 6.

Spoon a layer of sausage sauce, without any meatballs, into the base of a 30 x 20cm (12 x 8in) gratin dish. Cover with a layer of pasta, then a layer of sliced mozzarella. Make a layer of sauce with meatballs, distributing them evenly, then sprinkle with pecorino. Continue making layers in this way until all the ingredients have been used. Finish with a generous layer of sausage and meatball sauce and grated pecorino.

Bake for about 15 minutes. Serve immediately.

200g (7oz) Italian sausages

6 tablespoons extra virgin olive oil

5 tablespoons white or red wine

100g (3½oz) tomato purée

300ml (½ pint) water

4 fresh basil leaves

salt and freshly ground black pepper

200g (7oz) pecorino cheese, freshly grated

50g (2oz) fresh breadcrumbs

1 garlic clove, finely chopped

2 tablespoons finely chopped fresh parsley

200g (7oz) minced lean beef

1 egg

500g (18oz) penne

2 mozzarella cheeses (about 120g/4½ oz each), thinly sliced

serves 6–8

COLD PASTA

07

When our daughter was in her early teens and we used to spend time at Porto Recanati near Ancona, her friends would often invite her to eat with them on the beach on Saturdays. The variety of different cold pasta dishes that the friends brought, always fascinated me – they were not at all as we know cold pasta, which is usually always teamed with mayonnaise. And then I discovered the reason. Ancona and nearby towns had had, pre-second world war, a large Jewish community. No Italian can go a day without pasta so the Italian Jews evolved cold pasta dishes to eat on Shabbat when they were not allowed to cook. Their pasta dishes had spilled out into the rest of the community.

Penne con Zucchini all'Aceto Balsamico

Penne with Courgettes and Balsamic Vinegar

300g (10½oz) courgettes

4 tablespoons extra virgin olive oil

1–3 tablespoons balsamic vinegar

salt and freshly ground black pepper

1 bunch of fresh basil, shredded

2 fresh mint sprigs, chopped, plus few leaves to garnish

250g (9oz) fresh penne

100g (3½oz) feta cheese, diced

2 eggs

serves 4

Balsamic vinegar is made from the cooked concentrated must of white Trebbiano grapes, which have been harvestsed as late as possible so as to take advantage of every last bit of summer sun. It is aged in casks of different woods, first in oak, then chestnut, cherry, ash and, finally, mulberry. By law, it must be aged at least ten years. Some very old vintages are available and in Italy they are prized like good wine. It is a dark brown vinegar with a fluid, syrup-like consistency and a very aromatic fragrance, sharp but sweet. Try it sprinkled on very ripe, halved strawberries with a little sugar, as they do in Modena where this vinegar originates.

Wash and dry the courgettes and cut in half lengthways. Slice fairly thickly. Heat 2 tablespoons of the olive oil in a large non-stick frying pan and add the courgettes. Stir-fry for a few minutes, then remove from the heat. Splash with balsamic vinegar, season with salt and pepper and scatter with the shredded basil and chopped mint. Set aside to cool.

Hard-boil the eggs by lowering them into boiling water. When the water returns to the boil, let them cook for 10 minutes. Plunge them into cold water and peel before cutting into 6 pieces.

Bring a large saucepan of lightly salted water to the boil and cook the penne until al dente. Drain, toss a few ice cubes into the pasta to stop the cooking process, drain again and spread out on a clean tea towel to drain further.

Put the pasta in a large bowl, dress with the remaining olive oil and a little balsamic vinegar. Add the cold courgettes and stir in. Scatter over the feta cheese and egg wedges and garnish with mint leaves.

Serve cold.

Ⓥ

Insalata di Pasta con Pomodori e Capperi

Pasta Salad with Tomatoes and Capers

The caper plant arrived in Italy thousands of years ago and has been flourishing ever since. The most famous capers come from Pantelleria, an island off the west coast of Sicily, where the hot sun is ideal for cultivation. The buds are picked every three or four days from May to August, and each plant produces about 5kg (11lb) of capers a year.

Finely chop the basil, garlic and capers (this can be done in a food processor), then add to a bowl, combine, and pour over the olive oil. Set aside to marinate for at least 6 hours.

Bring a large saucepan of lightly salted water to the boil and cook the pennette until al dente. Drain, toss a few ice cubes into the pasta to stop the cooking process, then drain again on a clean tea towel.

Put the pasta in a shallow salad bowl, add the tomatoes, caper dressing and chilli flakes and toss well.

Serve topped with pecorino shavings.

12 fresh basil leaves

4 garlic cloves

4 tablespoons small, salted capers, washed

2 tablespoons extra virgin olive oil

450g (1lb) fresh pennette, conchiglie or any other small pasta shape

24 cherry tomatoes, halved

½ teaspoon chilli flakes

pecorino cheese shavings, to serve

serves 6

Insalata di Pasta, Carciofi e Uova

Pasta, Artichoke and Egg Salad

juice of ½ lemon

12 globe artichokes

500g (18oz) fresh farfalle

150ml (¼ pint) mayonnaise, preferably home-made

3 eggs, hard-boiled, shelled and quartered

salt and freshly ground black pepper

1 tablespoon finely chopped fresh parsley

serves 6

Use only the small variety of artichoke for this recipe – viola or violetti. As these varieties have no hairy chokes, or none to worry about, once the outer leaves have been removed, the whole artichoke can be eaten.

Fill a large bowl with cold water and add the lemon juice.

To prepare the artichokes, remove and discard the outer leaves and wash the artichokes under cold running water. Cut each one into quarters and immediately drop into the acidulated water so they do not discolour.

Bring a pan of salted water to the boil. Drain the artichokes, add them to the pan and boil until tender, testing frequently with the point of a sharp knife to avoid overcooking. Drain and leave to cool.

Meanwhile, bring a large saucepan of lightly salted water to the boil and cook the farfalle until al dente. Drain and set aside to cool.

Toss the pasta with the mayonnaise to coat, then add the artichokes and mix well. Put into a large serving dish, decorate with the egg wedges, season with salt and pepper and sprinkle with the parsley.

Serve cold.

Ⓥ

Tagliolini Freddi alla Salsa di Pomodoro

Tagliolini with Tomato Sauce

Ippolito Cavalcanti, Duke of Buonvicino gave the official seal to pasta al pomodoro in his book *Cucina Teorico Pratica* (1839). Up until then, it had been passed on by word of mouth as a part of the Neapolitan oral tradition. Cavalcanti's recipe was simply a timballo of vermicelli and tomatoes. The tomatoes were sliced raw and the vermicelli was uncooked, seasoned with salt and pepper, layered alternately in a dish with oil or butter poured over, then baked. This is a Jewish recipe which comes from the Venetian ghetto. The sauce has a slightly sweet and sour taste owing to the vinegar.

Heat the olive oil in a frying pan and cook the garlic until pale golden.

Add the tomatoes, vinegar, salt, sugar and chilli flakes and simmer for 20 minutes or until the sauce is thick. Mix in the parsley.

Meanwhile, bring a large saucepan of lightly salted water to the boil and cook the tagliolini until al dente. Drain and mix with the tomato sauce. Serve at room temperature.

3 tablespoons extra virgin olive oil

2 garlic cloves, finely chopped

1 kg (2¼lb) tomatoes, peeled, seeded and diced

2 tablespoons white wine vinegar

salt

3 teaspoons sugar

a generous pinch of chilli flakes

1 bunch of flat leaf parsley, finely chopped

450g (1lb) fresh tagliolini

serves 6

Ⓥ Ⓥ

Fusilli alle 'Ciliegie'

Fusilli with Cherry Tomatoes and Mozzarella

330g (11½oz) fresh fusilli

100g (3½oz) rocket, rinsed, stalks removed

1 garlic clove, peeled

4 tablespoons extra virgin olive oil

1 fresh chilli, seeded and finely chopped

16 ripe cherry tomatoes, peeled and halved

salt

200g (7oz) *mozzarella di bufala*, diced

serves 4

Mozzarella di bufala is made from the milk of water buffalo, but you can use cows' milk mozzarella instead. It is a fresh, nourishing cheese that goes well with both pasta and tomatoes. It is traditionally produced in Central and Southern Italy with the biggest concentration of buffalo herds to be found in marshy fields around Caserta.

Mozzarella started to be made on a large scale in the 1500s, but it is recorded that the monks of San Lorenzo in Capua gave bread and *mozza* to the hungry who came to their door in the third century. Mozzarella was originally called *mozza* – the word derives from the Italian verb *mozzare*, meaning 'to cut off'. It is made from curdled milk which is then drained to eliminate the whey. The curd is cut into small pieces and ground up in a type of mill. At this point it is placed in hot water and stirred until it takes on a rubbery texture. The cheese-maker then kneads the cheese with his hands until it is shiny and smooth. He then lops off *la mozzatura* (sufficient mozzarella) to make individual *mozzarelle*. These are placed in cold water and then in brine for a couple of hours. Then they are ready to eat.

Bring a large saucepan of lightly salted water to the boil and cook the pennette until al dente. Drain, toss a few ice cubes into the pasta to stop the cooking process, and drain again thoroughly.

Tear up the larger rocket leaves. Rub a large serving bowl with the garlic, then discard the clove. Place the rocket in the bowl and drizzle with the olive oil. Add the chilli and tomatoes and season with salt. Toss well to blend evenly.

Add the cooked pasta and mozzarella and mix through. This dish can also be served hot, in which case do not add ice cubes to the pasta.

(V)

SWEET PASTA

08

The following sweet recipes are fun to try. They certainly make a talking point. Savanarola, a Dominican monk and religious reformer who lived in Florence during the fifteenth century, would no doubt have been very disapproving of these recipes. He castigated the Florentines from the pulpit saying, 'It's not enough for you to eat ravioli, it's not enough to boil it in a pot and eat it in it's juice, you have to fry it in another pan and cover it with cheese!' They eventually burned Savanarola at the stake but *not*, we have to add, for grumbling about pasta.

Torta al Rum

Rum Torte

FOR THE PASTA FROLLA

200g (7oz) plain flour, plus extra for dusting

100g (3½oz) icing sugar

pinch of salt

100g (3½oz) butter

1 egg

drop of vanilla essence

FOR THE FILLING

300ml (½ pint) milk

1 vanilla pod

1 cinnamon stick

4 egg yolks

3 tablespoons sugar

1 tablespoon cornflour

50ml (2fl oz) rum

4 x 9cm (3½in) meringue

200g (7oz) fresh, uncooked tagliolini

25g (1oz) butter, melted

1 teaspoon freshly ground cinnamon

serves 4–6

In 1533 Catherine de Medici arrived in France to marry the future King Henri II, bringing her own cooks with her. At her wedding feast, one of the courses was a pasta dish dressed with meat juices and cheese, and another dressed with butter, sugar, honey, saffron and cinnamon: one savoury, one sweet.

Make the pasta frolla using the method on page 18. .

Roll out the pasta frolla on a lightly floured surface and line a 23cm (9in) quiche tin with it. Set aside in the refrigerator for 30 minutes.

For the filling, pour the milk into a small pan and add the vanilla pod and cinnamon stick, bring to just below boiling point and remove the pan from the heat. Set aside for 5 minutes. for the flavours to infuse. Strain the milk and discard the flavourings.

Using a balloon whisk, beat the egg yolks with the sugar until pale, then beat in the cornflour. Gradually beat in the flavoured milk. When it is fully incorporated, pour into a small pan, set over a low heat and bring to the boil, whisking constantly for 1 minute or until thickened. Remove the pan from the heat, stir in the rum and pour the custard into a bowl. Set aside to cool to lukewarm.

Preheat the oven to 180°C/350°F/gas mark 4.

Remove the dough-lined tin from the refrigerator and pour the lukewarm custard into it.

Break up the meringue roughly and scatter over the top. Mix the tagliolini with the melted butter and scatter over the top.

Bake for about 40–50 minutes. Remove the tart from the oven, allow to cool and dust with the cinnamon before removing from the tin and serving.

Ⓥ

Torta Taglioni

Taglioni Tart

FOR THE PASTA FROLLA

250g (9oz) flour, plus extra for dusting

150g (5oz) icing sugar

150g (5oz) butter

pinch of salt

2 eggs

drop of vanilla essence

FOR THE FILLING

200g (7oz) almonds

250g (9oz) sugar

grated rind of 1 lemon

700g (1½lb) apricot jam

250g (9oz) fresh tagliolini

60g (2½oz) butter, diced

FOR THE SYRUP

40ml (1½fl oz) alchermes

65ml (2½fl oz) rosolio

25ml (1fl oz) almond liqueur

45ml (1¾fl oz) water

serves 6–8

Rosolio is a liqueur of water, sugar and alcohol, perfumed with essence of herbs or flowers. The most popular kind is made from red rose petals, perfumed with orange flowers, cinnamon and cloves. It was a much-favoured drink of the gentry during the seventeenth and eighteenth centuries, and only went out of fashion recently. Alchermes is a crimson-coloured liqueur which gets its colour from cochineal. It is made with spices – cinnamon, cloves, nutmeg, mace, coriander – and jasmine and iris. If you cannot obtain alchermes, use sweet Marsala instead. The colour will not be so effective but the taste will still be good.

Make the pasta frolla using the method on page 18. Leave to rest for 3 hours.

Roll out the pastry on a lightly floured surface to a thickness of 4mm (⅛in) and use to line a 28cm (10½in) quiche tin.

To make the filling, coarsely chop the almonds in a food processor with the sugar and grated lemon rind.

Preheat the oven to 150°C/300°F/gas mark 2.

Spread the base of the tart case with the jam, add one-third of the almond and sugar mixture and cover with half the tagliolini. Add half the remaining almond mixture, the remaining pasta and then the remaining almond mixture. Lightly press and dot with butter. Gently fold in the edge of the tart slightly. Cover the tart loosely with a piece of aluminium foil and bake for about 1½ hours or until the tart is a deep golden colour.

Meanwhile, make the syrup by combining all the ingredients. When the tart is cooked, remove it from the oven and drizzle the syrup evenly over it. Allow to cool, then chill in the refrigerator for 4–5 hours before serving.

Ⓥ

Pizza Dolce alle Sette Sfoglie

Pasta Cake

In Anna del Conte's book, *Gastronomy of Italy,* she writes of a very similar version of this dish which she obtained from a lady who lived in Puglia. It has a Christmas flavour about it, although Anna calls it a Renaissance flavour. My mother, who loved making pasta and sweet dishes, used to make it for our restaurant in the early 1970s.

Make the pasta (page 10), adding the sugar at the same time as the salt and the Marsala with the eggs. Roll out as thinly as possible. Cut into 12.5cm (5in) squares.

To make the filling, place the apricots and sultanas in a bowl, add the rum and set aside to soak. Blanch the almonds and walnuts in boiling water for a few minutes and remove the skins (this is easy for almonds but a bit fiddly for the walnuts).

Dry-fry the hazelnuts in a heavy frying pan over a high heat, shaking the pan frequently. Transfer the hazelnuts to a food processor. Dry-fry the almonds in the same way until a light golden colour and add to the food processor with the walnuts, then chop finely.

Transfer the nuts to a bowl, add the spices and grated chocolate and mix thoroughly.

Combine the apricots, sultanas, rum, raisins, currants, candied peel and ginger in another bowl. Add the orange flower water and rose water and mix well.

Preheat the oven to 170°C/325°C/gas mark 3.

Line a 23 x 18cm (9 x 7in) lasagne dish with aluminium foil and brush the foil all over with olive oil. Cover with a layer of pasta, without overlapping it. Drizzle over some of the remaining olive oil. Sprinkle with 2 tablespoons of the nut mixture, some of the fruit mixture and with small spoons of jam. Continue making layers in this way, until there are seven layers of pasta. Finish with a layer of pasta.

Brush the surface well with olive oil, cover the pasta with a piece of aluminium foil, sealing it well under the rim of the dish and bake for 1½ hours. Test if the cake is ready by inserting a skewer into the centre. If the pasta offers no resistance, it is cooked.

Remove and discard the foil. Leave the cake to cool in the tin.

Place a large sheet of foil on a tray. Place the tray over the tin and invert the cake on to the tray. Peel off the foil from the base of the cake, if necessary. Wrap in the new foil and leave to mature for at least 2 weeks, preferably a month.

FOR THE PASTA

275g (10oz) Farina 0 or strong plain white flour, plus extra for dusting

salt

75g (3oz) caster sugar

2 eggs

1 tablespoon dry Marsala

FOR THE FILLING

12 untreated dried apricots, cut in strips

50g (2oz) sultanas

3 tablespoons rum

50g (2oz) hazelnuts, skinned

75g (3oz) almonds

50g (2oz) walnuts

½ teaspoon ground cloves

¼ teaspoon freshly ground white pepper

½ teaspoon ground ginger

1 teaspoon ground cinnamon

60g (2½oz) bitter chocolate, grated

40g (1½oz) raisins

40g (1½oz) currants

200g (7oz) candied peel

2 pieces of preserved ginger, cut into small pieces

1 tablespoon orange flower water

1 tablespoon rose water

200ml (7fl oz) extra virgin olive oil

350g (12oz) damson or any other sharp fruit jam, preferably home-made

serves 10–12

Ⓥ

Crostata di Tagliatelle

Tagliatelle and Almond Tart

Make the pasta frolla following the method on page.

Butter and flour a loose-based 23cm (9in) quiche tin. Roll out the pasta frolla on a lightly floured surface to a circle a little larger than the tin. Line the tin with it and set aside in the refrigerator until required.

To make the filing, beat the egg with the sugar until pale and creamy, then add the almonds, candied orange peel, orange flower water and melted butter. Mix well together, adding a little milk if the consistency is too thick.

Preheat the oven to 170°C/325°F/gas mark 3.

Remove the dough-lined tin from the refrigerator and pour in the almond filling. Fold in the edges of the pastry. Scatter the pasta on top of the almond mixture.

Bake for about 40–50 minutes. Remove the tart from the oven and brush the surface with melted honey. Set aside to cool, then remove from the tin and serve either lukewarm or cold.

FOR THE PASTA FROLLA

200g (7oz) plain flour, plus extra for dusting

100g (3½oz) caster sugar

pinch of salt

100g (3½oz) butter, plus extra for greasing

1 egg yolk

grated zest of 1 lemon

FOR THE FILLING

1 egg

100g (3½oz) sugar

100g (3½oz) blanched almonds, finely chopped

75g (3oz) candied orange peel, finely chopped

1 teaspoon orange flower water

25g (1oz) butter, melted

1–4 tablespoons milk (optional)

150g (5oz) fresh tagliatelle

2 tablespoons melted honey, for brushing

serves 10–12

Ⓥ

Pasta Fritta con Miele

Fried Pasta with Honey

500g (18oz) fresh capellini

450ml (16fl oz) sunflower oil

200g (7oz) clear honey

6 tablespoons lightly crushed pistachio nuts

Gelato de Fior di Latte, to serve (see below)

Alchermes, to serve

serves 6–8

This sweet pasta comes from Sicily but the nuts and honey reveal an Arab influence.

Bring a large saucepan of unsalted water to the boil and cook the capellini until al dente. Drain and form into little nests by twisting the pasta around a fork.

Heat the olive oil in a deep pan and fry the nests until crisp. Drain on kitchen paper and transfer to a serving plate.

Heat the honey with the pistachio nuts and pour over the nests. Serve with gelato di fior di latte and drizzle alchermes on top, if you have some.

Gelato Fior di Latte

Ice Cream

150g (5oz) caster sugar

350ml (12fl oz) full-fat milk, chilled

150g (5oz) single cream

¼ teaspoon vanilla essence

serves 4

This is an eggless ice cream, so it's suitable for people who cannot eat eggs.

Stir the sugar in a little of the cold milk until it has dissolved. Mix all the ingredients together and freeze in an ice cream machine according to the manufacturer's instructions. If you don't have an ice cream machine, pour the ice cream mixture into a bowl and place it in the freezer. After 30 minutes, when it is beginning to set, remove it from the freezer and beat well with an electric beater or hand blender to disperse any ice crystals, then return it to the freezer. Repeat this 2 or 3 times, then leave until set firm.

Ⓥ

Index